R I S E

ABOVE DISRUPTION

A Journey of Self-Realization

*that will motivate, inspire, and give
you hope to find your own Zen.*

Khaled Khorshid

ISBN: 978-1-913969-39-4

DEDICATION

To my late father, who taught me to be myself and be first, daring, and different.

To my mother, who is the source of warmth and peace in my life.

To my brother, who is my backbone and my comrade.

To my two kids without whom life is not worth living.

To my best friend of all time to whom I owe a lot.

To my friends without whom I couldn't have survived.

And finally,

To the woman who showed me how to love, gave me hope, and kept me grounded.

PREFACE

The purpose of writing this book is to document my journey of finding inner peace after months of multiple traumas that left me in a dark tunnel clinging to dear life. I'm not a writer. In fact, this is my first attempt at writing any book. I really am an average guy who got so disrupted by one trauma after another, merely a few months apart, that I finally decided to write about my experience in an effort to ease the pain and learn about myself in the process.

Yes, I went to hell and back in the span of a few months, and I am lucky to be in a position to tell you what happened on this wild journey. I will tell you how I overcame financial hardships, the terminal illness of a loved one, the abrupt end of my 22-year marriage, and finally, cancer.

I'll explain what went one with my feelings and thoughts while trying to surf the high waves of change. How I managed to convince my brain that there is light at the end of the tunnel, and how I turned my vision of hope into reality. I knew that there was a light at the end of the tunnel. Then I started to see that light. It took a while to get out of that tunnel, but I got out as a new person — sharper, wiser, stronger, and more resilient than ever before.

My intention is to share with you the methods that have helped me overcome my fears so you might, too, find your own way to rise above any disruptions you may face in life. Throughout this book, I have shared things that have helped me find my inner peace and allowed me to lift myself up in the darkest moments. I hope after reading this book, you find yourself in a better mood than when you started. I sincerely think our view on life is a direct reflection of our own attitude. Enjoy reading!

If, after reading this book, you feel like contacting me, you can reach me at info@khaledkhorshid.com.

I would greatly appreciate your honest review of my book on Amazon, Google Play, Good Reads, Barnes & Noble, and Apple Books. Feedback is a gift, and I look forward to receiving yours.

Contents

Page Left Blank Intentionally

1 - INTRODUCTION

"If we had no winter, the spring would not be so pleasant: if we did not sometimes taste adversity, prosperity would not be so welcome."

- **Anne Bradstreet**

I need you to know that what you're about to read is the documentation of a journey of self-discovery that I embarked on without any planning. In fact, I did not recognize that I was on that journey until I was deep into it. In fact, as I'm writing these words, I have an emotional overflow – I don't know why, but I have tears in my eyes, realizing how profound that journey was and still is.

My tears are not of sadness but of awe from realizing the difference between the person I was and the person I'm now. I think they're tears of relief, tears of how much pain I felt, and tears of reliving the waves of changes that impacted my life. I might also be feeling the huge weight of putting my feelings and deep emotions out there in the open for the public to read in this book. I'm happy now, don't get me wrong. Ironically, in retrospect, I was convinced that I was also happy before that journey. What will interest, and I hope, help you, is reading about how my journey evolved. It is a real person's account of rising above drastic changes. I'm a person who shares a very similar background, values, beliefs, dreams, and aspirations as the majority of human beings. It is my account of how I handled disruptions that rocked the cornerstones of a stable, average, and mostly happy life.

Anyone of you reading this book will relate to who I am. Most of you will see parallels and similarities between our lives. But none of you will have the same journey I'm having.

Note: I say "I'm having" because the journey did not end yet. I'm in a stage now that is past all the turmoil and pain. In a stage of peace! Well, more about that later, but just remember when I started writing this book, I was in the middle of my journey.

This is unique because you'll get a first-hand account of the evolution of my self-realization journey, almost step-by-step. You will notice differences in the depth of my writing and the profoundness of my thoughts, analyzing my deep feelings and reasons behind my reactions.

How Would You Rise Above Disruption?

It might sound simple, basic, or cliché. It is all about knowing yourself and getting to know your *real* self! How would you know your real self? By trying to dig deeper and finding out which image of *you* are you trying to maintain, keep, or portray in front of yourself and the people around you.

Is it *yours* or someone else's image you're trying to reflect? Are you in complete synchronicity between what you see, what you feel, what you think, and what you do? Is your heart, body, mind, spirit, and soul aligned? Are they turned to the same wave? No one is fully synchronized all the time, but for you to rise above disruptions and hardships, a minimum level of synchronicity is required. Let me be clear and honest.

The only reason I found myself on this journey of self-discovery is the huge wake-up-call I got when my life turned upside down with no warnings. The five hardships that happened to me disrupted my world within weeks. This made me confused, hurt and baffled on a quest to find my peace of mind. When the world came down on me, I started asking myself many questions:

* Why is all of this happening to me at once?
* Why what I'm feeling is not synchronized with what I'm thinking (I feel so much pain, yet my mind believes that it is so unfair what's happening to me, yet it's happening)?
* Why are my feelings not matching my thoughts and my actions?

The conclusion was that a minimum level of synchrony is needed between what I'm feeling, seeing, thinking, and doing. The bigger the gap between them, the longer the journey to rise above disruption, and the more pain endured until inner peace is realized.

Finding my synchronization is one of the most significant outcomes of my journey. In reality, the act of writing this book helped me in articulating and surfing through my journey. It was my way to help get aligned with my inner and outer self. It was my way out of disruption.

Your way out of your traumas might be painting, singing, writing poetry, helping the homeless, teaching children, caring for the elderly, etc. It is yours and yours only! When a person goes through major life changes, aftershock, grief, and self-pity, they reach a moment of truth when they ask why so and so is happening to them. When I wanted to answer this question, I started to self-criticize and analyze by asking myself who I really am. I re-evaluated my values and belief system. I looked at the way I perceived myself and pondered upon how others perceived me. It may be a bit twisted, but your brain is really capable of much more complicated analysis. While analyzing, I reached the revelation of not being in synchronicity.

I realized that all this time, I was trying to be a role model for everyone around me: the best dad, the best son, the best husband, the best boss, etc. It's a human need to be in pursuit of perfection, wanting to be the best at anything and everything. Similarly, I was pursuing this ideal image, which I perceived I had always wanted for myself. The reality is, it was only in "my head". It was not real. I was far from being perfect, far from fitting my ideal self. I did not face myself directly to fix it.

I became an expert in finding convincing excuses for myself to justify why I fell short of reaching my ideal image. It was always someone or something else; the economy, business, or environment - you name it. I was like an ostrich. I wanted to look my best — which I wasn't — and I stuck my head in the ground to avoid seeing the gaps between reality and my perception.

Once I reached this conclusion, I went back to question everything about my life: my values, belief system, parents, upbringing, relationships with friends and family, career, and marriage.

Being the pragmatic, logical, calculating, and politically correct self that I was, as far back as I can remember, I had to set aside my brain and give more room to my heart and emotions. In doing so, it was unavoidable to revisit old emotions, wounds, feelings, and experiences. I began discovering what made me happy, sad, or satisfied, and then I started writing this book.

Once I began to be at peace with myself, of my deficiencies, and accepted that I have flaws because I'm human, it all became simple.

I had to get grounded, and I realized that writing about all this was the best way to do that. I got the space I needed while writing. Then, I started reading what I was writing.

While reading my own words time after time, I realized that I was just another human being with flaws and that I was far from being perfect. I'm not giving you a guideline to follow. I'm only describing how I ended up dealing with my traumas. I believe it will serve as a reference to find your own way to get over your own hardships. This would afterward become *your* own way of rising above your disruptions. My life was disrupted five times in a span of two years. One disruption followed by the next, from my business shutting down and erosion of life savings, to the spiral sickness of my mother, to the loss of my house, to divorce and ending on being diagnosed with cancer.

Yes, I had to deal with these five traumas almost simultaneously. One of these traumas is tough enough to put a person down. Imagine having five! I did it, and so can you. My path might be different than yours, but in the end, you will survive. Trust in that.

2 - THE CORE

Who Am I?

My name is Khaled Khorshid. I was born in Cairo, Egypt, to a father who was one of the early computer engineers in his generation and a mother who was a foreign languages translator. Following my father's career, we moved to the United States in the late 1980s. I spent most of the first half of my life between Michigan, Ohio, and Illinois. The exposure to different cultures, backgrounds, and geographies shaped my personality and character early on in life. Diversity is part of my DNA, and it is the key success factor of any country, company, or institution.

They say, like father like son, so when it was time to choose what to study in college, I chose to major in computer science. After completing the degree, I got recruited by a well-reputed consulting firm. Life was very kind to me as it landed me in my dream job. Everything was normal, and life was defying its principle of contradicting linearity. My career seemed to be on track. The line on the graph of my growth was elevating at a satisfactory pace. Life continued being generous, and in that regard still is, helping me find a wife with whom I had two adorable children. By the year 2000, my career took another swift turn, and I found growing career opportunities in the rapidly growing telecommunication sector in Africa.

I was content with life and everything in it. Luck was always on my side, as without it, I would never have been that successful early in my career. Luck has its own way of functioning; it brings you in the right place at the right time.

Today, I teach Digital Strategy in a reputable university, and I advise companies on change and business transformation. Speaking of change, I found that a popular interpretation of the word change is 'fear'.

Now, why does fear come to our mind when we hear the word? Is it because we discourage any emotion or activity that is dissimilar to our existing trail of habits or routines? Or is it because we fear change might make things worse, instead of making them any better.

No matter what the reason is, change and fear should always be considered separate realities. For many people, the change could be an exciting endeavor. It's not something you are immune to, and so you had better come to terms with it instead of showing any resistance. I'll try to show you a different perspective on looking and dealing with change using examples from my own journey.

Frames of Reference

My parents' relationship is, by default, my reference for family, love, trust, and respect. I was blessed to be raised by a very compatible couple. My parents were in love long before they got married. The exchange of intense emotions never goes in vain, and so, eventually, they tied the knot. Marriages require a balance between differences and similarities.

Both my parents are emotional individuals. They regularly exchange positive emotions. Since my childhood, I found them very communicative, which is very important at every level. Communication is what mitigates differences and sheds light on the similarities. They showed immense love towards my brother and me. Speaking of balance, my mother was the conservative one in their relationship. My father, in comparison, was more open to new ideas. This contradiction was very useful as I had introspected both sides.

They were both college graduates, and since they had grown up in the same environment, their beliefs, morals, and virtues were aligned. My maternal and paternal grandparents were also college graduates, so they came from educated families. Education lays the foundation of my positive, can-do mindset. My parents' education greatly influenced the approach they acquired to raise us. Although they were a good match, they had plenty of differences that enriched their relationship. For instance, my father was a dreamer. He looked beyond what he could see and always aimed for the impossible. I believe my mantra of being first, daring and different was a direct influence of his personality and the way he raised me.

My mother, on the other hand, was a realist. She always kept her expectations as realistic as possible. In addition to these attributes, as you could tell, my father was a risk-taker. He was always attracted to adventures fueled by his will to explore. He constantly looked for ways to improve his life, his skills, his career, and reach his higher self. My mother, on the other hand, preferred not to take many risks. She thought that being on the safer side was always wise and predictable. Mom and dad supported each other in every way they could. Whether it was the small things like buying furniture or important career decisions, my father always respected my mother's advice and opinions. It was the purity of their intentions that they shared such honest emotions. Faith and trust were always there; one was the strength of the other. There were many things I learned from my parents' marriage, and the first of them was stability. They created an environment of love and respect and painted the perfect picture in mind for a happy married life. Later on, during my divorce trauma, I realized that these "default beliefs" were the strong forces that made me resist and reject my wife's request to get the divorce.

These forces delayed my acceptance of this major disruption. More on that later. You might be wondering how this is relatable to your life. Let me solve this riddle for you. When a person grows up in a family that constitutes its structure on strong values and relationships, they are trained to carry those values with them. It enables them to implement these values later on in their life and create a warm environment for others around them. The environment we keep our kids in is the environment they learn to create. Growing up, I did not quite notice, but now that I look back, I find the pattern of all my relationships to have a prominent similarity. In all the women I have dated (or considered for that matter), I have always looked for a worthy relationship. There isn't much success I have had in this department, but it sure reflects the impact of my parent's marital life on me. Among the many things they instilled in their children, an important one was to have strong faith.

By faith, I do not mean religious values or choices but the belief that good things in life can happen to you. If you believe good things will happen to you regardless of how irrational it seems, believe me, they will happen to you. It is what I was taught at a very young age, and it has never left me. It has helped me a great deal to rise above complex circumstances. This unwavering belief in "good" is what tells me that no matter how difficult the present is, there will be a far better tomorrow.

My father always used to tell me that money is only a tool. He would advise me never to consider money as an objective or destination. His words have always stayed with me. You might have heard of the phrase 'happiness lies in little things,' but have you pondered over its meaning? Now relate this phrase to 'money can't buy you happiness.'

Money and happiness are two ends of the same perspective. Money is important because, indeed, happiness can be a victim of your bills and rentals. It's not just vital for you, but also the people who are dependent on you. Well, everyone knows it's important, but what many lack is an insight into its significance.

There is no harm in working on the ways to expand your income, not unless you compromise your priorities. See, money is a temporary entity – it comes and goes. It is the people who are important, and hence, when you find the opportunity to increase your earnings, always weigh both things; the price you're going to pay versus the financial gains.

In 1998, I was offered a job by a tech company with a higher salary and title. I was content with my job then, but I considered the offer. The new job would've entailed a lot more travel and long trips away from my young family. My wife was pregnant with our first child, and being present with her was more important to me than the extra salary.

I turned the job down because sharing this special period with my wife was much more valuable than the additional money and a bigger title.

We are all capable of adopting principles, which have the potential of bringing our life in the right direction. You might already have some of these traits; all you have to do now is identify them. We have great energy and potential, but what we lack are intent and discipline.

The discipline one must have within their self is not governed or observed by extraneous stimuli, but it is an internal quest. It is a constant struggle of improving your persona and refreshing your charisma.

The principles one acquires during their childhood and adolescence stay on throughout their life. In my case, they include valuing family relations, preserving a structured life, looking for worthy relationships, keeping faith (staying positive and being hopeful), understanding that money is only a tool (not an objective), and being content yet always thriving for more.

Growing Up

My brother is my best friend. He is very special to me, and I cherish him and the times we spent together. I feel we are two faces of the same coin. We got each other's back. He is my rock and my mirror. Having a sibling is always fulfilling. The bond you create and the relationship you develop outweigh all the apparent complexities. While growing up, my brother would often challenge me and interfere in my regular affairs. Back then, it seemed terrible to have him constantly bothering me, but today, when I reflect back, I am grateful to have him in my life.

As we grew older, we became great friends; there was a time when we were roommates after finishing college. The time we spent living together solidified our relationship, and we became very close. As a child, making friends is often perceived as easy as borrowing a colored pencil. As we grow older, our friendships can take a back seat to our technologically driven lifestyles and busy schedules. We become so caught up in our family and job obligations that we put friendships aside and lose some of the most important relationships in our lives.

It's important to always bear in mind that it's often our friends who are best able to keep our feet on the ground when the world around us is spinning out of control. And it is during life's most challenging times when we are most desperately in need to engage in real communication, and we feel the need to be heard and understood by someone we can call a friend.

Friends can lean on each other, and there will be times when one may lean more than the other will. When you're prepared to go the distance, though, you will see that it all balances out. You may be one of those people who are good at giving to others but are reluctant to let your friends love and care for you. You might be afraid of being weak, vulnerable, or dependent.

Think about this. If you don't let your friends give to you, it's a one-way relationship, and the deepest part of you is not really in it. You may feel safe, but this is not a full relationship, and it's not a true friendship. My friends have taught me that true friendship requires both giving and receiving. Give as much as you can and be gracious in accepting what they're giving to you.

3 - THE VOICES

*T*he voices in our heads aren't just existent in one form. They speak to us in different ways, each potent to bring change in our everyday lives. However, the magnitude of change is totally dependent on how we nurture them. Self-talk is just as involuntary as is the blinking of eyes, and as per the law of nature, everything is there for a reason.

The voices can psyche us up for an important occasion while helping us prepare for it at the same time. Our guilt trips of not reconnecting with our loved ones, driven by our inside voices, work just the same way. Among the three different scenarios mentioned above, what do you think is common? In my opinion, their projections are subject to our attitude. Simply put, you tell yourself what to do.

It might all sound very philosophical, but it really is not. Let's speak of the science behind it. As a matter of fact, science is better at explaining the influence of inner voices. It tells us how these inner voices impact our mental health and helps us understand ourselves better. Once you research the subject, you will be surprised to know that various researchers have proven the similarities between inner and external speech.

A lot that is happening in our bodies is the reflection of what's happening in our brains. When the inner voice whispers in our heads, there are subtle muscle movements in the larynx muscle to complement it. For those of you who don't know, the larynx is the upper part of our throats, that we use to speak out loud.

So, the larynx is active even when we do not intend to speak out loud. In this chapter, I want to introduce you to the voices we have in our heads in a way you might not have thought of before. Sometimes, a slight change in perspective is all that is needed to understand things better. Anyhow, when we are going through conflicts and emotional dilemmas, the voices in our heads have a vital role to play.

I have categorized these voices into three personas, or you could consider them as three different voices, three characters in your mind. All in all, the idea of their distinction is what has to be picked. I have named the first persona as 'Frank.'

Frank is the frank side of my mind character. It encourages me to always go with honesty and keep things transparent with my peers and friends. It's also the processing unit of the brain as it helps me in processing information and making decisions not driven by impulsive reactions, but analytical evaluations.

My decisions are mostly based on logical explanations, and it's Frank's responsibility to search for them. I need Frank all the time, throughout everything.

The second persona is 'Teddy,' my heart. First, I need to explain some fascinating facts about this essential organ. Amongst ancient civilizations, many have considered the heart to be the center of sentience, thought, and emotion. Science, psychology, and medicine have made us understand that it is the brain that is the center of all thought, emotion, love, and instinct, to name a few.

Those who still champion the heart being capable of thought do not say that the heart is like the brain but feel that the heart is capable of some basic thought and emotional feedback. Some of these will quote the Bible as it does mention in several places that the heart is the seat of thought and emotions. This literal interpretation cannot be applied today with the influence of modern science. In the age that the Bible was written, the heart was the center of thought. This view was appropriate then. However, the people that feel that the heart has a certain brain-like function, as do some doctors, tend to base their argument on the basis of experiences of some heart transplant recipients. These experiences are all along the same lines, as the recipient has felt certain emotions, changed certain behaviors and taken on some of the characteristics of the donor[1].

To lend further credence to the debate, recipients are never intentionally given any info on the donor other than some very basic details. What we do know is that the heart, like several other organs, does contain neurons. The heart has about 40,000 (compared to several billion in the brain).

Psychologists once maintained that emotions were purely mental expressions generated by the brain alone. We now know that this is not true — emotions have as much to do with the heart and body as they do with the brain. Of the bodily organs, the heart plays a particularly important role in our emotional experience—the experience of emotion results from the brain, heart, and body acting in consent. Recent studies define a critical

---

[1]Monemian, S., Abedi, H., & Naji, S. A. (2015). Life experiences in heart transplant recipients. Journal of education and health promotion, 4.

link between the heart and brain. The heart is in a constant two-way dialogue with the brain — our emotions change the signals the brain sends to the heart, and the heart responds in complex ways. However, we now know that the heart sends more information to the brain than the brain sends to the heart. And the brain responds to the heart in many important ways. This research explains how the heart responds to emotional and mental reactions and why certain emotions stress the body and drain our energy.

As we experience feelings like anger, frustration, anxiety, and insecurity, our heart rhythm patterns become more erratic. These erratic patterns are sent to the emotional centers in the brain, which it recognizes as negative or stressful feelings. These signals create the actual feelings we experience in the heart area and the body. The erratic heart rhythms also block our ability to think clearly.

One important way the heart can speak to and influence the brain is when the heart is coherent - generating a stable, sine-wavelike pattern in its rhythms. When the heart rhythm is coherent, the body, including the brain, begins to experience all sorts of benefits, among them greater mental clarity and intuitive ability, including better decision-making. Although the heart and brain are in constant communication, we can intentionally direct our heart to communicate to our brain and body in beneficial ways. When I experience sincere, positive emotions, such as caring, compassion, or appreciation, Teddy processes these emotions, and the rhythm becomes more coherent and harmonious. This information is sent to Frank and the entire body neurologically, biochemically, biophysically, and energetically. When I fell the shift into a coherent state to bring Frank and Teddy into harmonious alignment, I feel I have more access to intuition. It can take a little practice to do this on demand, but it gets easier and quicker the more you do it. Most of us are naturally inclined to make decisions from the heart. I am no different; passions and emotions fuel my decision-making process.

Teddy is my heart, and no matter how much it contradicts with my brain, i.e., with Frank, I still can never ignore it. As humans, we are bound to be confused, which is mainly because Teddy and Frank are ends of the same line. They are never destined to meet. There is a constant battle going on between the two; at times, the mind wins, and other times, the heart triumphs. The reason behind the conflict between Frank and Teddy is the different approaches they have.

They view a thing or situation with two completely different perspectives. It's like one tells you about the pros, while the other focuses on the cons, but it's not as simple as it sounds. Pros for the mind are often cons for the heart and vice versa. I have to make the decision on which side to choose. To be fairly honest, I tend to rely on my heart more as compared to my mind. That said, logical factors are important to me, and that is how Frank often manages to have the decision in its favor.

The third persona is my soul, and I call it, well, 'Soul.' Any word or name might not be able to suffice its meaning or do justice to its character. It is the most sacred part of our consciousness, or is it our consciousness? Or conscience? In any case, it is what makes us human.

There is a different kind of struggle that my soul brings with it. It is a thrust or temptation to become a better version of myself. You might find the analogy humorous, but I find it accurate to understand the role of the soul. Like every software needs an update with time, our soul brings an update to our mind and body. It does so through our experiences. I usually think of myself as the soul in the sense that I am what my soul is. Soul inspires me to protect and save myself while working on ways to elevate it at a higher level. You must be wondering how one can gauge self-development based on their soul. The answer to it is pretty simple; the elevation of our soul is visible in our behavior and actions. For instance, people who are satisfied with life are the ones who've never stopped in their struggle. They are the ones who give their best in every situation. So, if you want to have a peaceful soul, you will continually have to focus on improving yourself.

Mind, heart, and soul are the three personas that combine to define the voices in our head. The challenge that I later realized is to have the three voices in synchronicity, each keeping the important role they play in my life. They are the three parts of me that needed to be aligned to rise above my disruptions.

Whether I am in a difficult situation or a pleasant one, I rely on Frank, Teddy, and Soul. Frank and Teddy help me in weighing the situation while Soul makes the final call. Soul provides the balance that is required for decision making. I believe whenever I ignore Soul, my decisions are impulsive and bring me into unwelcome circumstances.

4 - CHANGE

What Is Change?

*Y*ou wake up in the morning, look at the time and realize you overslept because your mobile alarm did not go off as planned. You're late to an important client meeting to close a major contract. You're shocked, you're angry, you frantically jump out of bed into the shower, and without missing a beat, you're in a cab or an Uber hoping to make it on time.

What you experienced that frantic morning was a small brush with *change*. Your planned, predictable daily morning routine was *disrupted* by an unexpected event (alarm error), causing you havoc and forcing you to find alternatives to go back *on track*.

All human beings deal with change following the same exact four steps SARA Change Model: Shock, Anger, Resistance, Acceptance. In the alarm example, you would probably start by saying something like: "What?! Why the Alarm didn't go off?" Then you'd become angry: "I'll be late for my meeting"! Followed by resistance, your morning has been disrupted. You'd say: "I get it that sometimes my mobile freezes, but I don't like it." Finally, you'd enter the acceptance phase of SARA by finding ways to make it to your meeting on time. Every person goes through SARA at each and every change or disruption that happens in their life, from a flat tire, missing a flight, losing a loved one, or being diagnosed with cancer. The person will have to go through each step SARA in the same exact order: shock first, then anger next, followed by resistance, and finally, acceptance. The duration each step would take is unique to every person depending on the actual disruption. You could be quick through the SARA steps if you have a flat tire, but it could take you days to accept the passing of your dog.

There is no right formula or checklist to give you to help you deal with change. What I tried to do throughout the book is to explain how I organically went through the disruptions and major changes that took place in my world. It's important to remember SARA to be aware of how your brain and emotions deal with change.

What Is Disruption?

There are currently 7.8 billion people in the world, and the number keeps increasing every minute. It has always fascinated me how each individual has a world of their own, how every single person has a story to tell, and how the universe speaks to us all in different ways. We are all different, yet somehow so *alike*. Life has never been the name of stagnancy; we all go through highs and lows in this journey. Ultimately what matters is that we stay firm on this belief that as the good days pass, so will the bad.

Just like how success and failure go together, so do life and *disruption*. The uncertainty in life is what makes it exciting and is exactly what makes it scary. Sometimes a moment is enough to drive you to success, and so is it sufficient to write the script of your downfall. If you are lucky at the moment, do not take this situation for granted. After all, life can challenge you with fierce moments, and before you realize it, you might already be past your destruction.

The textbook definition of *disruption* is a disturbance or problem that interrupts an event, activity, or process. It is synonymous with "interruption," which has a largely negative connotation because it is an undesirable or unplanned *change*. It is the action of preventing something – system, process, or event – from continuing as usual or as expected.

Change disrupts our lives. Disruption is when we find ourselves on a path and think we're unstoppable, but one event, just one singly event, changes our direction. The entire course that we'd chosen for ourselves takes a sudden shift, and all our visualizations come to a sudden, abrupt stop. Is this the end that we were destined to meet?

For example, think of a professional athlete who got their break and are doing tremendously well for themselves. One day, they get into an accident that prevents them from competing anymore. All their plans come to stagnation. It hurts, it is a change, but it might just be a learning experience.

Similarly, a corporate executive's life gets disrupted when he finds himself a victim of downsizing. In the process, he might lose his house, life savings, even his wife. He might be thrown out of his comfort zone completely.

His Mercedes would go, and his parents' older Toyota might become his ride; the huge house with seven rooms will go, and a small rented apartment will become his humble abode.

Everything Happens for a Reason

I'm a believer in fate as much as I'm a believer in working hard to reach one's dreams and aspirations. As much as I believe in providence, in predestination, in the existence of a divine decree with God's will, I'm also convinced that striving to improve my life and prosper act as fuel for achieving success. They say the more you practice and work hard, the luckier you get. There is a fine line between both beliefs, which can become fuzzy at times.

Conflicts do erupt in my mind, and Frank goes in circles, sometimes trying to identify reasons for events or things that happen to me. That's who I'm, many times a believer in one thing and its opposite. Depending on the situation and the internal battle between Frank, Teddy, and Soul, I find myself most of the time, when faced with life situations or evet, to concede to God's Will and tell myself its fate.

There is no better story to prove my point about fate than the story of escaping death after passing on the airline's invitation to volunteer and take an earlier flight from Detroit to NYC. It was during spring break. The flight was delayed with plenty of empty seats. The airline wanted to offload some passengers from my flight to the earlier one.

Although it was tempting to arrive early in NYC and start my vacation earlier, I opted not to change my flight to reach on the planned time with my other friends. There was no point in arriving earlier and standing alone until they arrived. To my luck, good fortune, and *fate,* the flight I refused to take voluntarily, crashed on landing at NYC, killing half the passengers! If this is not fate, what is? It wasn't meant to be that I'd die that day.

5 - SKY FALLS

My career started in the mid1990s after I completed my MBA. I was recruited by one of the top consulting firms, and it was how I started my career in technology. It was the dot com era when the internet industry was a booming one. It gave me the chance to work on big projects with Fortune 100 companies.

I was gaining experience in a rapidly growing industry. The job market had a lot to offer, and so I was approached by various firms. On average, I had at least two to three job offers per year. My career took a steady start; the graph of my income showed a linear increase every year. The first fifteen years of my professional life were very kind to me.

I kept on juggling between job offers and switching as per my liking. However, my income wasn't the only thing growing; my personal and professional responsibilities increased just as much. I was at the top stair of my career ladder in 2008. At the time, I was the youngest CEO of a telecommunication operator in Africa. The telecom industry was growing day by day, and the opportunities to grow seemed endless even when I had secured the topmost position in the corporate hierarchy. The pace at which I was succeeding in my professional life made me feel invincible, feeding my ego to dangerous levels. My ego distracted me and fogged my vision, and soon enough, it created a blind spot in my perception. The blind spot was growing because I failed to keep myself grounded and remember that any industry will have a downturn, that growth is never perpetual, and that competition will soon intensify, and the economics will flip.

I was getting set up for a big fall from grace; it was still a few years away. In one of my jobs, I was the CEO of a group of companies in telecom and technology, which gave me great exposure to the media and the press. I was pleased with how my career was escalating, and all I could see was more success coming my way.

The higher I went in my career, the bigger the blind spot became, only adding to my ego. Nevertheless, it was fueled by fun and thrill, enabling me to excel and surpass my own limits. The period of my success in the telecommunication industry did come to an end in 2016, but it brought about a new beginning. I decided to start something of my own. I, with a close friend, created a company that had plans of targeting the telco space. How was I going to be more successful as an employee? I was the CEO, and hence for growth, I had to do something different. It was indeed logical to think of starting something of my own. When you have sufficient experience and knowledge, you are naturally inclined to start something from scratch – something that you can call your own. I was trying to fulfill a dream I had for years.

I was committed to and hoped that it would all work out. Subsequently, I invested all the money and expertise I had. I had built a decent network throughout the years with my career. I was a success story and wanted to make sure the final chapter of my professional life was the most inspirational one.

In all honesty, I do not regret any moment of this great run of a career. I've had my fair share of ups and downs, but those ups and downs still did not make me see the blind spot that was increasing. I was setting myself for the first disruption, without even knowing. Unfortunately, due to the market collapsing and a few other factors, my dream and vision remained unaccomplished. Things did not turn out to be the way I had assumed. It was the start of my disruption – the motivation behind writing this book and sharing my story. Although career disruption wasn't the first of its kind that I endured, it was very significant in changing my life 180 degrees.

I lost most of the savings as I had invested them in this company. It's not that the company wasn't in a complete loss, but it never entered the self-sustainability phase. After three years of spending my savings in the form of investments, I decided to close down the company. I would have never closed it if I had another option. Are you wondering what my first disruption was? Well, hold on, we will get to it.

My career suffered miserably, and shutting down the company had a huge impact on my ego, understandably in a negative way. Building my own company changed the dynamics of my life, bringing me to a point where restarting had become all the more difficult.

Failure is part of success, indeed, and I'm a true believer that you can't be successful without failing at all. Thomas Edison was asked how many times he tried to invent the light bulb. He replied that he made over a thousand attempts until he finally managed to light the bulb. This was when he said, "I did not fail 1,000 times but found 1,000 ways of how it couldn't be done," which became a famous, evergreen quote.

Anyhow, the loss of my investment and bankruptcy together brought a very difficult time for me. For somebody who is motivated by achievements and known for meeting targets, it is very disheartening to go off track for a while and be unable to achieve targets they set for their own venture. It wouldn't be wrong to say that it was tough for me even to accept that I was not able to achieve my targets, especially when it was a business that I put all my efforts and money into.

I was not at all habitual of failing, let alone thinking about failing my own business. I gave my 100% to it, but nothing seemed to work. Now that I think of it, I realize it was meant to happen. It probably happened to make me familiar with failure and to help me learn the importance of failing. What made it all worse was that this was not the only bad thing happening in my life at the time; my personal life was just as stressful as my professional life.

6 - BROKEN ROCK

*C*hange is a natural process. A seed changes into a plant under certain conditions such as sunlight and adequate water. The little chapters we start in life are like the seeds. When we provide them the light of positivity, along with commitment, the seed grows into a healthy plant. However, there are times when the storm takes the seeds with them. It is a very critical situation; then, finding patience is soiling your seed. The storms represent the *disruptions*.

I was in the last phase of closing my company, so I had a lot of stress on my mind. It was 1:30 pm on January 20th, 2019, a time and date I will never forget. I was in a meeting with my partner, planning the shutdown of our company when suddenly my phone rang. It was a phone call, after which life remained no longer as I knew it – my life changed.

Mom had called in great pain, asking me to come to her house immediately. It turned out she had fallen walking down the hall and had broken her hip joint. I rushed out of the meeting straight to her house. Her left hip joint had met with a sad fate. It was tough for me to see my mom in excruciating pain. She was in her early 70s, and so recovering from the injury was not going to be easy. She felt powerless in the painful situation she was in, and I desperately wanted to do something to ease her pain. I rushed her to the hospital. Now, a ball joint can never repair itself naturally, and replacing it with a platinum ball is the only solution.

The older the person, the longer it takes for the artificial ball to adjust to the body. There can be plenty of complications pre-and-post-surgery— our body functions in an amazing, yet complicated way. Whenever a foreign element is introduced to our internal systems, it is not usually welcomed by our bodies. I was worried if mom's body was going to accept the artificially manufactured ball joint or not.

It sounds like a very convenient solution, but its complications make it a tough call. What happens when the body rejects the replaced ball? It can cause an infection that has the potential to be fatal. Let's say, as is in most of the cases, the body accepts the newly operated ball joint. The pain is unbearable, which lasts for days. I guess the pain lasts for a long time, and you just learn to live with it.

Replacing a ball joint means weeks and weeks of no walking. This meant that she would be totally dependent on my brother and me until the new joint adjusted to her body weight. Despite all the complications, we decided to go with the surgery. It was the only way forward.

Mom never had any medical problems in her entire life. She was the rock of the family, the source of energy, the best support system for not only my brother and me, but also for her brothers, sister, brothers-in-law, sisters-in-law, and her step-mother who raised mom like one of her own. In other words, she was the backbone of the entire family, who always kept things from falling apart. To see the *rock* broken was catastrophic with unimaginable consequences.

The procedure was performed successfully, and it took Mom almost three months to get back on her feet. For somebody as active as her, spending time in bed was a misery. She just wanted to push herself off the bed and get back to her daily chores. However, it was the immense physical pain that stopped her from doing so. She went through physiotherapy sessions patiently, waiting for it all to be over. She had started walking again with a cane, but within a few days, the tragedy re-occurred, and Mom fell again. It was the same hallway where she fell, but this time, she landed on the right side. Her right hip joint also broke, which meant she had to go through all of it again. Mom was mentally prepared to have the hip-replacement operation; again, it's what experience does to you. We knew that Mom's body had accepted the earlier joint, so the probability of acceptance of the new one was also high. Basically, she knew how to manage with it, but experiencing that pain again was not just a physical but also a mental challenge. Honestly, after looking after her for three months, imagining her bedridden had a profound emotional toll on me too.

On top of all that, I was stressed financially and then had to take care of mom's expenses too. I started to slip, slowly but surely, into the dark tunnel of hopelessness. Everything in my life was at a halt, as I postponed everything until my mom's recovery. It seemed like we, Mom and son, were stuck in a delusional loop. She is the most important person in my life. I have no regrets, and I am glad I was there for my mother in the time of need and was able to dedicate all the time that I had. It took her another three months to get back on her feet again. They were – till then – the toughest six months of my life as I had to support her in every aspect of her life. We are so engrossed in everyday life that there are mere moments when we reflect on the course our life has acquired. Being unable to get involved in any activity beyond my mom's recovery encouraged me to sit back and reflect on life. These ideas weren't naturally in my mind, but I forced them into my thoughts to gain strength. Life always plays its part, not allowing time to freeze, whether its moments of joy or nights of sorrow.

It wasn't until June that I started to come back to my routine life, as, by June, Mom had finally recovered from her second surgery. She was in much better shape. I thought the period from January through June was the toughest period of my life. Little did I know that it was not; it was; in fact, the beginning. I thought I reached the peak of my hardship and disruption, but life is full of surprises, isn't it?

7 - MONEY TROUBLES

*I*n the span of six months, I lost my company and life savings while supporting my mother during her illness. I barely got over these two disruptions when the third one found its way into my life.

I had to finance my kids' education, but there was nothing in my bank account that allowed me to do so. After giving it a lot of thought, and realizing there was no other way, I decided to sell my house. It was too much to handle. Everything was happening so quickly, and I was suffering at all ends. I was suffering as a businessman, a son, and now even as a father. I sold the house and made sure that my disruptions did not impact my children and family.

In the course, I realized the complexity of the college education system. Not everyone in America can pick the college they like unless you're entitled to a financial account that has a handsome amount in it. Yes, finances are not all that will get you there, but on average, most students cannot afford the college tuition fee. Paying for college while managing other expenses can be indeed very stressful.

College Education Made Luxury

Back in our time, getting into a college was way more affordable than it is today. If you disagree with me, just do a little research on the subject. You would be surprised to know that every year the tuition fee increases to over 3%. It's not that complicated. Just compare what the fee of any university was two years ago to what it is today. There has been an increase every year. I agree that a lot in the economy has changed, but why has the increase been exponential while the economic downturn slow-paced in comparison.

Education institutions have been prioritizing profits over purpose. Various universities have deep pockets to aid students, but not every student is fortunate enough to benefit from such financial aid programs. It is not only the students who suffer; their parents do too. When I think of it myself, my top priority was to ensure my children got enrolled in colleges of their will. They are both hard-working and passionate, so I had complete faith in their choice.

The only problem that occurred was the finances. I was already going through a lot, and my bank statement was deteriorating by the day.

No matter what, I had to make sure my children did not drop out of college only because they didn't have the money. The house was all I had, and so I decided to sell it. Now, if education isn't a luxury, why did I have to sell the most valuable asset to pay for it? I was in a position to surrender what I had, but several people out there have a more complicated situation.

People who have younger kids to take care of cannot sell all they have for one child. Then, some people won't just have enough to pay for their children. On the other hand, how do we expect children to pay for it? There are young, have no experience, and want to attend college to learn. They would have to start their career with liabilities. It takes years for college graduates to pay for their student loans. As I said, there are other expenses too.

The Struggle Is Real

Like every parent, I did not want to see my children face such crises, affecting their learning. I want to see them as successful people who inspire others around them. I wanted them to center their focus on education so that they excel to their potential. I was a good student myself and was taught the importance of education at a young age. Although my parenting is quite different from that of my parents, emphasizing on education was what we shared in common.

The top colleges and universities around the world are doing a fantastic job with the academics and teaching methods. Sharing knowledge is the noblest profession in this world, but commercialization or capitalism is tampering with its nobility.

There are over 1,500 colleges and universities in the US alone. Every college has several programs. There are thousands of students who get enrolled in these educational institutions every year. So, when education becomes a luxury, a huge number of students and families are affected. I was amongst the many who suffered.

If my company had been doing fine, I would have made the payments easily. I had never been as broke in my life earlier as I was at that point. I had been leading a comfortable life for years, and it did not just happen suddenly. I had worked hard for it. I had earned everything I owned. Maybe, if the financial disruption had exploited me gradually, I might have used the time to adjust and make peace with reality. You need to be slow and steady to climb the ladder of success, but the fall is quick. Life had gotten very difficult in no time, but my positive, optimistic, and hopeful side of my soul kept on convincing me that the dark night of disruptions was about to be over. There was so much happening in my life that I thought I had seen it all. A lot had changed in a few months, but I was fine with it, hoping that the commotions had finally come to a halt!

8 - The Divorce

Family Dreams

*E*very person has dreams and visions. We are all focused on achieving them, trying our best to follow the path that leads us to our goal. Nevertheless, nobody wants to walk that path alone. In times when the heat of the sun melts our soul, we want a partner that serves to be a cold gust of wind. When the night seems dark and terrifyingly silent, it's a relief to look by our side and find a person that brings brightness in our present. In short, sooner or later, we all want to settle down and tie the knot.

When I found the woman I later married, we were attracted to each other in quite a few ways. What drew us closer was what we shared in common. We were coming from similar backgrounds, so adjusting to each other's lifestyles was not that big of a task. It wouldn't be wrong to say that we even had a very similar sense of humor. Once we began to know each other, we realized that we were compatible in many ways. Our friendship made us believe that we needed to take things to the next level, and before we knew it, I was on my knee, proposing. I wanted my relationships to support my ambitions instead of opposing them, and in her, I found that support. But as they say, everything has an end. Life was not allowing me to take any break from its disruptions. One hardship was followed by another, giving me no buffer to heal my emotional wounds. The last thing I expected was my wife of 22 years asking for a divorce!

Let me tell you the story from the beginning. I wanted to start a family and replicate the environment I grew up in. I wanted to be having kids at a young enough age when I had the energy to keep up with their growing up. I've always wanted to have a large family, beyond two kids but less than five. Three or even four would be great, but this must be balanced with affording to raise them in the lifestyle I envisioned.

By the time I reached my late twenties, I've had a few serious but failed relationships. They all started with physical and emotional attractions of some sort, grew into passion and love, but they each failed for their own unique reasons. All along, the frame that I was following was that of my parent's relationship, love, and marriage. That was the ultimate picture I saw and lived within its positive outcome.

After failing a few times to find the woman I would want to marry, I started to question the formula I was using to find her. I then decided to give emotions and passion a second priority and gave reason and logic the upper hand. After all, the person had to have the characters, background, education, family upbringing, and values that I share and find essential to have. When I met my first wife, she satisfied the logical reasons to be my life partner.

She felt familiar as we had a lot in common. It didn't take us long to decide to take the plunge and get married. We married in Cairo among our family and friends then flew to Spain for the honeymoon, and a couple of weeks later, we settled in our new hometown, Chicago. Everything was smooth and easy-going. I was living the life I wanted.

The foundations of our relationship were built on mutual respect and mutual care. We weren't really madly in love, but we really enjoyed each other's company. I loved traveling, and so did she. We traveled the world together and shared great memories, having experienced so much together. Our honeymoon was quite amazing as we took a road trip to travel around Spain. We also traveled later on to France, England, Portugal, Germany, Switzerland, Holland, Italy, and Greece. We even traveled to the Far East, visiting Malaysia, China, and India. So, when I say we saw the world together, I mean it. We both wanted to enjoy life, and so we did. We watched movies together and attended carnivals whenever we had a chance to. Summertime was spent on beaches, and to sum it up - we were living a perfect and healthy life.

Even after we had children, when I had the opportunity to travel to Africa for work, I took my family with me. It was what led us to have friendships with people of different ethnicities and cultures. People who love traveling are usually foodies and love shopping. We were no different in this regard.

Days were passing like hours, and by the time we had been married for two years, we were blessed with a son. To be a father was a very significant moment in my life. It completely changed my perspective about life and everything in it. Before having a child, I focused only on what I wanted. Now, it wasn't just about me, but the little creature, who was my flesh and blood. This adorable little angel was dependent on me, and I had to make sure that I provided him with the best. My priorities changed as I began to spend more time with him. I had changed as a person. Two more years passed, and we were blessed with a girl. I've always wanted to have a daughter, and I still remember what it was like to hear the news that my second born was a girl. It was a very humbling feeling. I love both my children, each in their own way. One can never understand parenthood until they walk through its doors.

When I began raising my kids, I could relate to so many things that my parents did. I was able to understand why my parents treated me the way they did. I even found it funny in a way doing things they did that I criticized as a child. As a father, they seemed completely justified. They are things you can't understand unless you step in your parents' shoes. I am sure my kids today might disagree with many of the things I do, but when they grow up and have their kids, I'm sure they will only find themselves doing the same things.

The significance of having children supersedes everything else in life. It supersedes graduation from university, professional growth, and even marriage. It is because, in everything else, the result constructs or destroys your own life. In parenthood, it's not about your life, but the life you have brought into this world. In my opinion, having kids is one of the best gifts from God. To have them in your life and watch them grow is fulfilling. Nothing can bring more happiness to your heart than those rewarding, satisfying, and joyful moments you experience as a parent. Every phase of a child's life is special for parents. Now that my kids are teenagers, it's not that those moments of joy and satisfaction are scarce. Their accomplishments and smiles still soothe my heart. To have them in my life is the best thing that has ever happened to me.

Divorce

In a time of crisis, one would expect the spouse to be a pillar of stability and moral support. Amidst all the hardships I was going through in the past year, my wife – for fairness – had been supportive and compassionate. Yet, when she asked for an amicable divorce, I was profoundly confused, shocked, and angry.

I was angry because, in my mind, divorce violated the idealistic picture I build in my mind for family, stemmed from my upbringing. I was confused because we had no major differences, disagreements, or trust issues.

I was shocked because, for the first time, I realized that a wide gap of understanding existed between the two of us. When did this happen? How did we let it slip away? What went wrong?

They were all questions too late to answer at this point. She was adamant about her decision. My only condition was for the kids to live with me, for which she did not oppose, neither did the kids.

My divorce was a major change in my life that I had not expected at all. I was already having a difficult time dealing with the three disruptions that existed together. I felt tormented and even thought that fate was waging war against me.

Everything associated with my life was falling apart, and no matter how hard I tried, none of it seemed to get back in order. I had to handle the divorce, just as I had handled all the disruptions before it. We were moving to two new places instead of one and getting ready for kids to go to college.

I had to find myself a place big enough for my two kids and me. My wife was finding her own place. It was just surreal and unbelievably foreign. I felt it was a bad dream and that I would wake up from it. The impact of every disruption was greater than that of the previous one. The fourth disruption hit me the hardest because I hadn't expected my 22 years of marriage to fall apart. Whether or not we were happy together is a separate subject of discussion, but what was important was the fact that a lot had changed.

I spent many sleepless nights listening to Frank trying to analyze the reasons and rationalize why and what had happened. Teddy was hurting and crying out loud. Soul was angry, feeling betrayed, and unfairly treated. I couldn't sleep for days from the noises in my head. It felt like I was going in circles without knowing why. The struggle I had between Frank, Teddy, and Soul was getting intense by the day. There was a constant conflict happening between the three. There were never-ending debates, leading to unsatisfactory conclusions.

Looking back to my failed marriage, in all honesty, it seems by now that what my wife and I enjoyed the most during those 22 years were raising our kids more than we enjoyed each other alone. We both found happiness in seeing those two precious people grow between us. Unintentionally but practically, our lives revolved around their happiness, their activities, their fun times.

Then slowly but surely, nothing else we did alone was as fun or fulfilling as those activities and fun times we had with them. The fun and passion we used to enjoy alone slipped away slowly throughout the years and started to be a distant past that was harder and harder to bring back or rejuvenate. To be fair and honest, my first wife was a blessing in many ways. Our life together had its ups and downs, but at the bottom-line, it was fun, fulfilling, full of joy and great memories and unforgettable moments. I attribute her support to a big part of my career success. If she was as demanding as the average wife, I would've had a hard time balancing between work and family. She filled in for me plenty of times when my career required me to travel over 100 business trips per year! She was, by all means, my backbone and the rock I leaned on.

We had strong trust and common belief in the same values and life objectives that kept us from forgetting where our *true north* was. She was - and still is - the best mother for my kids. I thank her for raising our two kids the way she did. For all these reasons, and with all emotions aside, I still have respect for her even after she decided to continue her life on a different path then the one I expected.

The ending of every marriage may seem dramatic and negative, but I believe at the end and after all the drama settles, it might end up being better and positive. It was not easy on me emotionally to accept shattering my "default frame" that inherited from my parents for the perfect marriage. It took me a few months to accept that I'm a divorced parent of two. You can't run from reality, and with the positive mindset I've always had, I finally accepted it. It was a difficult journey, and I thought it was the toughest trauma I had to deal with, or I thought so!

9 - THE CANCER

Is It Real?

*A*mid all those changes and hardships, I realized there was something physically wrong with me. I began to feel weak and was also losing a lot of weight. I thought that I was losing weight because of the diet I was on and all the stress that I had. I had started intermittent fasting a few months earlier and assumed it to be the reason behind the weight loss.

I ignored my health, in the sense that I thought it was nothing besides physical and mental exertion. I started to feel lethargic, frail, and even strange. I would get tired by midday and had to take a nap to get some energy to continue with the day. I was having fevers.

I consulted my doctor, and he suggested me to go through some tests. The results were devastating as I was diagnosed with cancer. I was given the news a day after my 50th birthday. It was quite a birthday gift life had given me. As per biopsy results, I had Hodgkin's Lymphoma, which is cancer in the lymph nodes. This was my fifth and last disruption - the straw that broke the camel's back. I could not have imagined that the roller coaster of disruption would take everything away from me. At first, it was my mother's health, followed by financial crises, a failing business, and then a failed marriage. So, this rollercoaster ended by actually disrupting the very last thing that I had left, my health. None of my parents had cancer. My dad had passed away at a young age, but it wasn't due to cancer.

We didn't have cancer in my family history, and the diagnosis brought me into a state of shock. I always felt bad for my friends who had cancer, and then I began feeling miserable for myself. Sometimes, I don't understand why and how I got to the point that I did. How did I find myself in the middle of this disruption, and what did I do to deserve it?

My new path was strange and different from what my reality used to be. This new path didn't feel right, and so I cried. My emotions got the better of me; I missed my old house, my ex-wife, and my children. I missed the familiarity of my past life. I wished I had appreciated all of those things more when I had them. Right before my cancer was diagnosed, I was in a very dark place. I felt I was in the middle of a dark tunnel, without any hope of finding the light. I did not know how deep this tunnel was and felt that everything was slipping away. Every night, I would lay down in bed, wondering if I would wake up the next morning. I lived with this feeling for weeks and months. I would often cry, too, and not because of my miserable condition but from the constant contradiction inside my head. It was like my mind was being pulled from two different ends. Yet I assured myself that it was okay to be emotionally torn.

Life of a Cancer Patient

Hearing the word "cancer" has a profound effect. The word is heavy and frightening for all the reasons that might have visited your mind hearing it. The treatment, in most cases, is a long and tiring process. It's not only your physical health that is affected, but also your mental health. Even relationships with loved ones take a blow; in my case, I was all on my own. The person with cancer initially feels overwhelming support, but it doesn't stay that way for long as emptiness soon follows. The cancer patient experiences a void of conversation, empathy, social interaction, laughter, and debate. These are a few of the many natural expressions that we take for granted for most of our lives. When loneliness creeps in, it comes along with a flashback of the previous life, haunting your thoughts. You have nothing else. You don't have the energy to work or do normal chores, so you have plenty of time on your hands to dwell on the negatives. We all have fears when diagnosed with cancer. My understanding of cancer is not only based on my personal experience but also on other cancer patients that I met during chemotherapy treatments and in the hospital waiting rooms.

The regular appointments and treatments make you see familiar faces for a while. Some you stop seeing because they are further ahead for you in their treatments' schedule, and some you stop seeing because, well, you don't always find out why, and the reasons are not always good.

In those hospital wards, where the specialist doctors and nurses work, you get to become a bit of an expert yourself. I have undoubtedly learned a lot of medical terms, understood how bad cancer could be, and learned to know that it is a fight. I also learned, to my relief, that there are plenty of people who win their battles. It wasn't just me, so in that regard, I am not that unique. I realize that I am thankful for all that I have enjoyed and endured over my lifetime. I am here, living a full life. Honestly, it was something that I did not expect to happen. My doctor frequently told me that I had a short life expectancy.

Despite learning about improvements through the medical perspective and practices, it is still challenging to believe that you will survive, and the pain will go away. Sometimes, the pain was worse in my head than it was in my body. Cancer is a topic that so little is spoken about. You might have also noticed that television campaigns, articles in the press, and social media show cancer in a way that we are stopped in our tracks.

It is the purpose behind the campaigns to make the viewers think. So, we stop, think, maybe make our donations, and then, we move on in our heads. As soon as we move on with life, we forget about cancer. It does not happen because we are heartless or selfish. It is because we rightly need to focus on our life affairs.

As a cancer patient, the only people you can really talk to are the specialized medics. Even my own doctor, who is absolutely marvelous, could only provide me with limited details. It wasn't his job. We expect our doctors to know everything, but of course, a cancer specialist knows a lot more. As a cancer patient, the only other informed people you can really talk to are the ones going through what you are. Or else, it is their loved ones who tirelessly and dutifully accompany the cancer patient fighting this awful plight.

Not everyone has a companion by their side, though. Not everyone wants their loved ones to see the insides of these wards. Not everyone wants their loved ones to know the misery caused by cancer. Well, what is it? It's not a disease yet gets called that sometimes.

Cancer isn't something that can be caught, transmitted through touch, or spread through the air. So, social distancing is not going to make any difference. Although some can be passed on genetically, that's a whole different topic, which is well outside my understanding. What I do know from my own experiences and listening to first-hand stories of other cancer patients is that being positive is the only way you can live with cancer. It is the best coping mechanism, but it is adopted after a lot of hard work – by digging deep and finding positivity. I have surprised myself in being able to dig deeper than I thought I could.

But I also surprised myself in not being able to dig at all! There were times that I just ran out of steam, and that was so incapacitating. I have always been able to find solutions, whether in business or finances. I was the guy who motivated teams to achieve incredible results. I have mentored grown men, supported them to pull themselves up emotionally, to work hard, remain focused and positive. There was I, a blubbering wreck at times, not once, but on many occasions. Unintentionally, or maybe not, having cancer patients together becomes free therapy. These people are much more willing to talk about their experiences. These are shared experiences, after all. There is an unexpressed sense of understanding and knowing that you are sharing your thoughts, fears, and aspirations in a safe environment. I came across people from all walks of life.

It was, without a doubt, a humbling experience to be in the company of people from starkly different backgrounds – people who I would never have met personally or professionally. I received kindness, information, and survival tips from these strangers. A lot of them also brought a smile on my face through their humor. Can you believe that you can smile and laugh when you are about to get attached to drips and machines during your treatment?

The capacity of the human spirit astounded me. I surprised myself as I am not a natural comic. I have been way too serious my entire life. Whether it was studies, work, or family, I was always kind of a serious guy. Yet, I learned the full breadth of human kindness. I have learned to use humor and find it in the unlikeliest places. Something I never ever expected of myself, but that's how cancer changes you. We are lucky to live in a well-informed world. We have access to masses of information, which is easily available through our smartphones. What I learned, and I urge any cancer patient or their loved ones not to do, is turn to the internet for information about the disease. You will not find the right answers there. I speak not only from my own experiences but from that of others. Leave the internet alone!

Ask questions to your doctors, nurses, and other patients. The medics can help you through the medical aspects of your cancer, and you may also get a therapist if you can or join a support group. You must most definitely chat with your fellow patients when you turn up for tests and treatments. There is a wealth of information and support there. Use it, give it, and consider doing it your duty. What are we if we are not willing to share, even during our darkest moments?

For anyone suffering from cancer, my advice to you is to not worry or overthink what is happening to you and around you. Have faith in doctors and nurses treating you. Live in the moment and enjoy life as much as you can. Obviously, this does not mean that you participate in risky activities. Listen to medical advice that you have been given. These people have dedicated many years of their lives to learn what they know, and they are continually putting themselves through the learning process. They are sharing what they know so that cancer can be eradicated one day. In the meantime, respect and value what you have.

I learned that the most important thing is knowing about cancer, instead of running away from it. Getting familiar with such diseases enlightens you with the harm it can do as opposed to what you assume it would cause. It's just staying informed about your condition. It takes time to accept cancer mentally and to develop an urge to fight it.

Friends in Need Are Friends Indeed

Being diagnosed with cancer, I can tell that every segment of a patient's life is affected. My financial situation was already bizarre, and it was about to get worse. I have always been a social person, but the disease had consumed all my energy to meet people and stay busy.

My close friends never left my side. Their support during my illness was overwhelming. I couldn't have surpassed this trauma without any of them. They organized a meticulous schedule of actions around delivering home-cooked meals, daily visits, even driving me to my chemotherapy sessions. I'm forever grateful for each of them and will never forget how they brightened up the dark days of my illness. Such overwhelming support didn't help tame my fears when I become alone. Every time my friends left, and I became alone in my apartment, Frank would dominate my conscience. It was Frank's daily routine to present the "what-if scenarios," ending up with painting the bleak picture of hopelessness and despair.

When you begin to feel that you have grown weak, a sense of disparity rides over your soul. The human brain is an organ and is affected by cancer, just as the other organs are. It has a direct impact on a person's mental well-being. It felt that things were going to be this way forever, only if they weren't going to get worse.

The brain reacts to the situation, and you feel burdened by anxiety and depression. It is a critical phase, as it is when you decide to surrender or fight against it. For a while, I let my fear-fueled by Frank to take over my soul. I slipped into being convinced that the possibility of me waking up the next morning was slim.

Hope

Hope is the most vital ingredient in the will to live. It is an emotional state that encourages you to keep on living. It is what is needed to become successful in life, regardless of the situation. If you don't manage to nurture hope in your approach, you have given up on the will to live. Hope will allow you to adopt a positive attitude, hence strengthening your determination to survive. This is a nice academic explanation of the positive impact of hope in one's life.

But that explains the impact *after* hope is *found*. But how do you find hope in such a state of despair? I read self-motivation books during this period of my disruption, and most of them explained, with irrefutable proofs, the power of hope. But none of the ones I read told me how the heck do I find hope when I'm so deep down my dark tunnel?? I was lying on my back at the bottom of the tunnel seeing nothing but darkness! No light at the end, not even a mirage.

My Frank, Teddy, and Soul were so drained that none of them could even get an illusion or a wishful thought that an end is in sight! So, hope to me was a joke at this point. I reached a point that when one thought of hope flashed in my brain, none of the three voices in my head would even consider it. And that made me cry many times because I realized that I was depressed to the core. Have you ever wondered how hopelessness feels? This is it. I just articulated for you the feeling. However, I wish for no one to experience these miserable feelings. So how did *I* find hope? I didn't seek hope. In fact, when I was in this state of hopelessness, I was not thinking, meaning my brain was idle. Frank would only be concerned about my basic needs, eating, drinking, sleeping, etc.

You can say I was just "being." Maintaining the status quo, breathing, feeding myself, keeping warm, sleeping, waking up. I had little to no interest in anything around me. I often ignored calls from family and friends. I told myself, just be. So, to think about hope or seeking it was a far-fetched proposition. After weeks in this state, I started to get bored. Nothing new was happening. My fear of death did not materialize. I'm still in the dark tunnel with no light in sight. I asked myself, what's next? But I had no meaningful answers.

10 - THE DEEP DARK TUNNEL

How Deep Did I Go?

*W*hen I was at the deepest point of my dark tunnel, I experienced a disturbing thought. The thought that losing anything dear and precious to my heart did not matter as much as it did before. The feeling of sadness associated with loss was not there for me. I tested myself on many levels. I, one day decided to give up most of my clothes to charity, including those pieces that I held somewhat dear to my heart, and on many occasions, I refused to donate. I wanted to see if material possession in this state of mind mattered.

It did not. I gave up all my clothes except pieces for seven days' attire and three occasions (casual, sports, and formal). A second test came unexpectedly. I learned the news that a younger friend and ex-colleague passed away in a horrible car accident. While my normal me would be disturbed with such tragedy, I didn't. I sympathized with his family, but I cared less, which is unlike me! I even found excuses to avoid going to his funeral.

This state of mind was foreign to me. I stopped carrying about others and only focused on me. Even when my kids called from college, I pushed myself hard to be nice and engaging, asking about their classes and life. That signaled a new low I've reached in the tunnel! It's understandable to be in that mindset when faced with a life-threatening disease. But to me, it was new, foreign, and in many ways, sad.

I have been through near-death situations and would consider myself lucky to be able to tell you what happened in my journey of life. I want you to know how I overcame obstacles, how I managed to believe that there is light at the end of the tunnel, and how I managed to turn that vision of hope into reality. I must confess that those quotes seemed implausible. It seemed logical to me that knocks in life stay with you like a noose around your neck, or I was so wrong!

Is There Light?

In my darkest time, I believed there was a light at the end of the tunnel. Then I started to see that light. It took a while to get out of that tunnel, but when I reached the other side, I was an entirely new person. I became sharper, wiser, stronger, and more resilient.

Sometimes I did not recognize the reasons why I was right in the middle of disruptions. It felt weird trying to get to terms with reality. Everything was out of place and not where things, people, and emotions should have been. This was not what I had planned for. This was not how it was supposed to be, and above all, why me? I often wondered why I am on this path right now. What got me here? Why am I living in this new reality? It hurt because I felt like I had failed in everything. I believed I had failed in my business, my marriage, and even in managing my health. Loneliness was my only companion.

It's OK to Cry

I cried on my situation – how things changed for the worse. I just grieved over life and everything that I had. My tears and sadness showed how much I missed my old reality, even though I willingly took some of the decisions, such as ending my relationship.

What I missed were the symbols of my success and hard work! I missed my old house, even though I willingly sold it to pay for my kids' education. My son and daughter are my worlds, and I would do anything for them. My whole existence since my children came into my life has revolved around ensuring that they have the best of everything. I have tried to make sure they have the best opportunities in life, materially, educationally, and, most of all, emotionally. Life has taught me that crying and grief are good emotions. I did not want to accept all that had happened at the time. Weeping out your sorrows is the first step in accepting the situation. It is why grieving made a positive contribution to my journey of recovery.

Being sad is a strength, as you require courage to shed tears. It's not how we are conditioned to think, though, is it? Typically, we believe that we must be able to control our emotions, and crying is a sign of loss of that control. It most certainly is not! Nothing can be more valuable than the truth itself.

My crying was solitary. My experience of crying, up until that point, was watching others cry. It was infrequent and only occurred for a few minutes. My crying was on a whole new level to anything I had witnessed any other person do in real life or a movie. I was almost inconsolable. Not only was I grieving for all that I had lost, but I was also crying over my stupidity of not appreciating what I had owned. On reflection, appreciating material things that I had owned in the past was quite a folly.

At the end of the day, materialistic entities can never console one's soul. Material possessions are not that important. We all know that, but sometimes, we need to have a reality check to stop prioritizing and wanting materialistic possessions so much.

What is important is the strength of our character. What matters is if we can find reasons to laugh and understand that we have a purpose. It's the people we love that make our world beautiful. They are the people who matter to us and whom we matter to. It is essential to have a voice that is heard, but it is also vital to learn to listen.

It would have been beyond embarrassment had I cried in front of anyone else. Whenever you see anyone cry in real life, they are always apologizing for showing their emotions. You hear them make comments, such as *"I'm so sorry to do this in front of you"* and *"I'm so sorry you had to see that."* The responses in return are often something like *"it's okay," "don't worry about it,"* and *"It's not a problem."*

In reality, we feel uncomfortable because we feel useless, as we are unable to stop the person from crying. We want the crying to go away somehow. Crying is considered an act of shame in public. It is not as it is, in fact, a logical recognition of what is happening in a person's life. I never thought that I would think this way, but there is a lot that life teaches us. Crying is therapeutic. It is almost like a cleansing of emotions and negative thoughts. I was surprised that I felt better after crying, and after some time, it became less frequent. My resilience started supporting me without me even realizing it.

I had lost all that I had; my company, work, wife, house, and health. They were times when I felt absolutely worthless and helpless. It was what created room for self-realization. I actually did start to find out who I truly am. I did not realize that deep inside my soul, there was gratitude for being alive, resilience to accept all that happened, acceptance for what God has put me through, and relief for having nothing to worry about.

Yes, strangely enough, I felt relief. I found myself thinking, *"What's the worst that could happen? Death? So be it. If I die, I'll be relieved from this pain, and if I continue to live, life cannot get any worse than it is. Let's be grateful!"* Even though I gave myself this pep talk, I kept drifting from moments of despair to this positive approach about what my fate could be.

My despair thoughts were, *"What? Be grateful? Look at yourself; you're miserable, you lost everything, you have cancer, you are alone, you have nothing!"* It was a constant battle of negative and positive thoughts – a battle that did not seem to end. It was draining my limited energy levels, but I couldn't stop myself. The cancer was incredibly, extremely demanding, as it exhausted me physically and emotionally.

My friends and family were quite supportive when I was fighting cancer. They rallied around me, giving me so much unexpected support and overwhelmed me with love and motivation to get through this difficult time. Then, as time went by, their support waned. Not because they didn't care, but because that's how life is – happening. Cancer, on the other hand, is not like a common cold. It sticks around for a long time!

Cancer treatments are time-consuming, and there is no straight line of progress. It can't be managed like a project at work, tamed like a pet, or nurtured like a child. Medics are still learning about the intricacies of all the different types of cancer and the nuances and measures to cure this awful health condition. People have their own lives to live. I suppose that seeing someone not improving might be disheartening or uncomfortable for most people who are around cancer patients. It's a bit like when someone suffers the bereavement of a close family member or friend. People just do not know what to say. Natural human emotion is that if something is wrong or someone is in trouble, we put all hands to the pump to fix the problem.

For most of us, the problem is that the task of fixing the death of someone and curing someone of a serious health condition such as cancer is outside of our skillset. So, it makes people stay away. Gradually, the calls become less frequent. Then, you don't get invited out to parties and celebrations. It's so uncomfortable for most people to cope with that. They do nothing rather than doing something wrong, which is more painful. Honestly, it is perfectly understandable.

Let me tell you, you will find a strength that you never knew you had. Trust that strength and trust in your ability to remain strong. You are not weak, and you need to tell yourself that over and over again. No matter what has happened to you in your life up until this point, you always have the right to smile.

You will meet some amazing people, and your horizons will be incredibly broadened. You will come out of this a much better person. I did! I have heard other cancer patients say the same.

After all, it makes you think in a whole new dimension, and above all, it teaches you to value life. Remember my question about how to find hope. It's time to tell you how I found it inside the dark tunnel. It wasn't until the positive result of my first major checkup that a glimpse of hope started to tease my brain. At the completion of the first phase of my treatment, I did a major full-body scan, and my doctor confirmed that the possibility of my survival was now above 90%! This was the only time the brain, heart, and soul started to feel hope. I could hear the voices of Frank, Teddy, and Soul arguing in a positive tone about hope and that light is indeed at the end of the tunnel.

11 - THE SUPPORT NETWORK

You Don't Choose Family, But You Choose Friends

*H*aving friends is vitally important to one's mental health and to the quality of one's life. To live and to love are inseparable from each other. Friendship is an opportunity to love, to learn about yourself, to mature as a human being, and to open up to the full experience of life. To seek true friendship, you must have the courage to risk all that you are.

You must have the courage to walk through your fear of emotional intimacy and let another person know who you really are on the inside. On a very practical level, you must be willing to invest the necessary time and effort to develop, nourish, and maintain the bonds of a strong relationship.

According to my friends, I'm a source of positivity, optimistic vibes, support, and honest advice. I was comfortable with giving my friends what they wanted. I was seldom open or comfortable asking for support or expecting it. I had a tough time with the unfamiliarity of receiving the overwhelming support they poured on to me when I was diagnosed with cancer. I did. I resisted opening up to them and spilling out my fears and vulnerabilities. Now I understand that my ego was in the way. My ego painted my perfect picture of the strong, cheerful, never weak-hearted me. I resisted opening up, and my close friends knew it.

They saw through me, and two of them confronted me, and I listened. When they left my house that night, I reflected on what they said. My ego created another blind spot that, over the years, was forgotten. I blocked the flow of my emotions towards my friends. Friendships can and do change. There has to be enough freedom and independence in your relationship for the growth that is a normal part of human development.

Be flexible enough to adapt to different ways of relating to each other. Marriages, children, careers, interests, and extended family constantly impact the daily structure and flow of our lives. This is where the effort comes in. You can find ways to keep the relationship alive and strong if you are willing to be creative. Having established the significance of friendship, I do often wonder if friendship is a gift that many of us sometimes take too much for granted.

The fast pace of modern life seems to leave many people with little time for those closest to them. Friendship can often be perceived as either a luxury (i.e., it is time consuming but doesn't yield any tangible result) or a burden (i.e., friends can sometimes be quite demanding).

In times of personal disruptions or transformation from one life chapter to another, your love for yourself supersedes any other love, even to the people closest to you! Have you had best friends who were inseparable become a second priority to starting a professional career or a new family? The relationship changes its dynamic. Your time, attention, and energy get routed to a more selfish pursuit of happiness.

The comforting fact is that most of your close friends pass through the same (you would hope), so it becomes a natural transition of things. It doesn't diminish the love, respect, and long history you've had with these close old friends. Still, it pauses the interactions and camaraderie and saves it for future periods when your life situations become convenient to relive those friendships. Throughout the years, you'd keep in touch and stay updated on each other's' life events. And at times of crisis to any of them, you all congregate back around the person in need.

This is when true genuine friendships come back alive. They pick up exactly where they left off. Certainly, our collective obsession with work and career can often lead us to neglect our relationships with friends and family members. Not only can the desire for professional success put a strain on our most important relationships, but it also leads us to put less meaningful professional relationships ahead of personal friendships.

While there is nothing wrong with aspiring for professional success and developing a network of business contacts, I have come to appreciate the well-known fact that at the end of our lives, no one ever regrets not having spent more time in the office. Of course, practically everyone would have liked to have spent more time with friends and loved ones.

Part of the reason for this notable decline in the perceived value of friendship may be related to technology, which paradoxically has made it much easier to connect with people via email and applications like Facebook and Skype, but which also keep us at home, often choosing to nurture virtual relationships over face-to-face friendships. Undoubtedly, computer technology and television are playing a far greater role in mediating the way we interact with people.

Movie rentals long ago replaced the popularity of a card game with friends as home entertainment with friends. While I do believe that this steady decline in the value we place on friendship is not a figment of my imagination, I do have a suspicion that the global economic slowdown and the COVID-19 pandemic could be playing a role in reversing this trend. Perhaps it is only my wishful thinking, but maybe this economic crisis is teaching us that there are things more valuable than a corner office and the latest home entertainment center? Humbled by forces beyond our control, are we now coming to realize that friends are the best marker we have for success in life?

In some stages of my life, my love for myself took over and superseded my love for my close friends. We've all experienced the disruptive times of the COVID-19 pandemic. It's during such times when your love for survival and wellbeing made you stay away from family, let alone best friends.

The impact is even multiplied if you happen to be passing through this pandemic while in the middle of turning to a new chapter of your life. That's what happened to me. I lost touch with a few friends and pissed-off a couple of my old best friends because I prioritized my happiness and wellbeing over theirs. I didn't do it intentionally. I simply couldn't find the time, energy, nor patience to cope with their needs during that period of my life. It seems unfair to them. It's unfortunate, but I subconsciously decided that my "cup" was overflowing, and I needed to empty it. As selfish as it may sound, I needed to transform to a new me, and I couldn't do it without emptying the cup of emotions, social obligations, and time commitment to be able to fill it again fresh on my new life priorities.

Deep inside, I know - and I'm sure they do too - that our friendship, love, and respect are unshakable; that our memories and history will never go away; and that we are always there for each other. Whether or not my hypothesis is true, there is certainly some very good reason for placing a greater value on friendship.

Beyond the enjoyment that comes with spending time with people we care about, our friends provide us with an important support network for more difficult periods in our lives. This is more evident in societies that place greater importance on social connections, strong family ties, and tribal heritage. Human connections in such societies supersede rank, experience, title, or qualifications.

Trust in such societies are more valuable than gold. Friendships in such societies are cherished and appreciated for life. It's who you know, not what you know. I grew up in such a society (Africa and the Middle East); they lived in a society with opposing norms (North America). From my view, social connections, friendships, and strong human ties supersede anything else.

Science has proved it recently. In 2006, a study of nearly 3,000 nurses with breast cancer found that women without close friends were four times as likely to die from the disease as women with ten or more friends. A study carried out by Australian researchers and published in the Journal of Epidemiology and Community Health showed that having friends around in old-age can do more for life expectancy than having family members around.

Other research has found that people who do not enjoy a strong social network are 2 to 3 times more likely to die at a young age than those who have this it. Like regular exercise and a balanced diet, maintaining meaningful friendships is a proven way to improve health, prevent disease, and extend life. Having lived and worked on three different continents, I have been blessed with many beautiful friendships. I fully understand how friendship often means different things to different cultures. Those friends that stand by us in good times and in bad do more than just helping us get over life's difficulties. Several studies have shown that friends not only help improve the quality of our lives but also keep us healthy, increasing our life expectancy.

Couldn't Have Made It Without Friends

My friends were the mere safety net that got me through the disruption that I experienced. Their presence was very critical and helped me a great deal in standing on my feet again. The younger ones reading this book might be wondering what the traits of a true friend are. When you think about friends, what is the first thing that comes to your mind? Think of one or many of your close friends to answer the question.

Loyalty? Does it ring any bells? Of course, it does. In short, friends are people you can trust, and to find a friend, always look for humbleness. A friend will never sugarcoat things to you, and if ever you find a person doing so, remember he is not your true friend. Friends are funny, they make fun of you, but at the same time, they are also very generous. They laugh over your mistakes, but also make sure you learn and get better. They mess around with your things but don't allow anybody else to mess with you. Real friends are truly a blessing. I was lucky to have all these values and characteristics in my buddies. Friendships are independent of circumstances.

Whether I was succeeding in life, miserably failing, or my finances were giving me a tough time, my friends have always been there for me. They are my safety zone, as I know that even if all my boats turn to ashes, my friends will always find a way to make me a new boat, stronger and more beautiful than ever before.

12 - RESETTING MY LIFE

Out of the Tunnel

*T*he stage of getting out of the tunnel was indeed the hardest of my journey. That's why I gave it more time to reflect on, explore, document, and illustrate—finding hope was hard, very costly, extremely painful, and draining. I subconsciously used many ways to find ways to see the light at the end of the tunnel. One of the ways I did so was by pushing myself to turn the chapter and start a new one.

If you think that your life is like a book, then each stage of this life resembles a chapter. You'll soon realize that turning a page is the natural transition from one chapter to the next. Turn the page, remember the previous chapter's lessons, don't get hung up on the details of that chapter.

It's gone, done, finished with all its joy and bitterness. I realized deep into my tunnel of darkness that all previous chapters in my memory are a heavyweight pulling me down deeper into the tunnel. I used to waste time reminiscing over the good times and regretting the bad ones. I soon realized that this is what Frank enjoyed doing, reminding me of how great life *was* and how painful it *is* missing those days. That's what he was created to do, keep feeding my ego happy memories when I was happy, rich, powerful, healthy in an effort to make me feel better. The result was the complete opposite, an explosion of emotions making Teddy sink deeper into agony and pain. Soul throughout all this gets overloaded and reaches the darkest points of negativity and despair. I stayed in this vicious loop for weeks and months on in.

I lost weight, appetite, and the will to fight back. This, for sure, impacted my immune system and exaggerated the pain I had from my illness. I lost 20kg in less than two months. I was in a state of free fall. It was much easier to give up and let the chip fall where they may rather than fighting back for dear life. I gave up. Frank kept on doing what it does best, giving me all the logical reasons regarding why it is likely that I'll die. It was pushing me to accept death.

"Just make sure your brother has the key to the house so he can come in a find you when you die." Write your will and letter of instructions to your son today because what if tomorrow never comes. Call your mother and kids as many times as you can to let them know how much you love them; you don't know when the last time you'll talk to them will be. Pray as hard as you can; soon you won't be able to." That was Frank's non-stop rambling. And Teddy agreed and went on a spree of self petty and hopelessness. Looking back, it was an ugly patch, a bleak chapter of my *book*. Deep inside, I knew that there is a chance this chapter will be over, and a new one could dawn, ushering new beginnings. I would toy with this idea every few days, the idea that I'm in an ugly chapter that will end soon. The chapter could be the last one in my book, and the end would be my demise, my fate, my time-to-go.

Or the chapter could not be the last, and that a new chapter could bring good things. This was my way of trying to *accept* hope. I say accept because, at this low point inside the dark tunnel, one doesn't have the mental or emotional capacity to see, let alone accept, hope. At least that's my experience — coming from a naturally "positive" guy. As time went by, the idea of accepting hope became familiar. Soon enough, hope started to shape up. Frank and Teddy agreed to give it a try.

Finding Hope

Hope is a unique feeling. It starts small, humble, simple, and reachable. Then it snowballs into dreams of idealistic and superhuman visions. It grows on you from a fuzzy, bright thing that is good and warm into a sharp, specific picture of how life would be soon. I lived through this emotional process and felt all its ups and downs. And I was convinced that I'm in a chapter that will end. You need to know that I believe of *change* as the core of my faith in God.

Everything changes in this universe. Sand, rocks, plants, oceans, animals, humans, beliefs, nations, everything, everything, everything changes. The only constant is the creator of the universe, the one who started it all and will end eventually, the supreme power, the one that never changes. To you, he could be Jesus, Elohim, Yahweh, Brahman, the Cosmos.

Believing in God as a default belief made my acceptance of change part of my DNA. And so, when hope was real, I accepted to turn the page to start a new chapter. I did not know what the chapter is about. All I knew was that I had to turn to a new chapter in an effort to find hope. To usher in a new chapter was to get rid of bad habits and adopt better ones. One was to be consistent in working out every day for 15 minutes in the morning. The second was start meditating— something I decided to learn a new skill that I wanted to do for long. Control my thoughts.

The Power of Thought

How many of your thoughts today helped you get towards your goals in life? How many of them hindered you? Are you in control of what you think? As I first learned the answer to these questions, I was shocked. Ask me just how little influence I had over the content of my mind a year ago, and the answer would've been zero. I look back on my life ever since I was a child, and I could clearly see that my mind had always been constantly wandering, distracted, and unable to focus.

The reason is that I've lived the way I have like any modern person, overstimulated. It was my lifestyle that had produced this unsettled mind of mine, which had now become nearly impossible to control, especially in times of trauma and disruption. For 20 years, I had been unable to recognize this phenomenon within myself simply because my mind had never been provided enough space to observe its own functioning.

There is a Swedish ex-monk who lived as a Buddhist monk for 18 years before returning back home to ordinary life just a few years ago. Upon his return, a journalist interviewed him and asked that after 18 years as a monk with hours of meditation every single day and no distractions, what's the one key insight that you took with home? His answer was, "I no longer believe in everything, I think." Sounds so mundane, and yet it's not. We are free to choose our own thoughts. You can become an architect free to construct your own life by design. For some of you, this idea might be familiar as it lies at the core of most meditation techniques.

Or perhaps it's a completely new one having yet to enter your mind. Well, regardless of your current standpoint, I humbly ask you to suspend any disbelief or belief. Whether you are a corporate CEO or a surfer, I invite you to enter an open state of mind. Now we find ourselves in a world where, for the first time in history, more people are dying from eating too much than eating too little, more people are committing suicide every year than are killed by war criminals and terrorists combined.

Starting with my generation onwards, we were raised from the very beginning of our lives to crave stimulants, and the world we live in is an obvious reflection of this. Think of anything we do like watching movies, eating ice cream, listening to music, going shopping, the list is endless. All of these are consumer commodities. They are produced as a response to human need. We have lost control of how we used it and have ultimately let them gain control over us and how we think. This was to the highest degree true for me and my past behavior. Whether you are a tech billionaire, a Buddhist monk, a military officer, or a high school teacher, you are (to some degree) being unwillingly dictated by your own thoughts but also free to change that.

The American psychologist and philosopher William James said that "Thoughts become perception; perception becomes a reality. Alter your thoughts, alter your reality." Basically, what I got out of his quote is that the quality and character of the world I live in are nothing but a reflection of my own minds. The only way to influence the world I live in is to learn how to influence my Frank. I'll share with you the two methods I stumbled that helped me stop thoughts from controlling me and take charge of Frank and thereby reality. It's the realization from my journey of 5 traumas I passed through.

Meditation

The first method or tool that helped me control my thoughts is Meditation. My long-time best friend from school became a meditation guru – he grimes every time I call him guru, but to me, he is! He has been talking to me about meditation for at least the past five years. I would listen but took no action. After passing through one trauma after the other in the span of a few months, he came to me one day and did an intervention.

He almost forced me to start meditating. I didn't need to be forced really; I was convinced that I needed to take the leap of faith and submit my logic at the door and let the power of the spirit and higher self-take its course.

His point was that I needed to start meditation now. I badly needed to synchronize my heart, mind, and soul. I started by developing a habit of meditating for just 15 minutes at a time four days a week, and that changed my life in many ways. It is, by definition, the art of developing mindfulness. It's practiced by consciously directing and maintaining my attention on an unstimulating object such as the breathing and doing this for a length of time.

This practice calms my mind and makes it less prone to overreaction, more rational with higher-performing, but the ultimate goal of meditation is to start objectively observing the mind. Let me give you a visual example of what I mean. Imagine yourself a web made up of thought, every thread a possible thought path leading to different places. After some meditation training, one is able to identify thought patterns, see where they will lead, and choose to take another path, and this is what happened to me. I started to see which one of my thought paths led me too excited and had done so for so many years. I was actually able to direct my thoughts towards something constructive instead.

As I gradually learned the structure of my own web of thoughts, I became able to actively predict which thought will lead to which emotional state. That allowed me to actively choose states such as calmness, serenity, and high focus over stress, anxiety, and anger. It is, in theory, quite clear. But then again, it can only happen as the mind is provided enough space and silence without being constantly stimulated.

Choose What Goes In

The second method that I found helpful in controlling my thoughts is to stop feeding my mind bad information. The saying that you are what you eat certainly applies to food, but have you ever thought of the notion of bad information having the same effect, making us mentally unhealthy, obese, and addicted. In this age of information and unprecedented junk data, load enters our minds every day and this junk data than influences our minds. It affects our values. It creates our needs and desires and even how we think. It's our responsibility as individuals to carefully feed our minds with selected input, and that input them if chosen wisely, will produce this desirable mental environment in which we can start to understand our minds properly enough to control them.

Is it constructive for me to be bombarded daily with newspaper tabloids of death, sex, fear, terrorists, and disease? I started to choose my media source wisely. I uninstalled many news apps from my phone to reduce the negativity. I left Facebook groups and pages that fed me such unhealthy data. Such sources are seldom designed only to transmit information.

More often than not, their primary objective is selling ads by sparking my interest using catchy headlines fueled by fear, which happens at the direct expense of fact. Social media is a brilliant tool when used right, yet so catastrophic when abused. It is not the harsh traumatic, or horrible events themselves I should fear. The most important factor for my survival is my willingness and ability to control my reactions to those events. The third method that I found helpful in controlling my thoughts was reading. I've read many books throughout my life, but

I've always felt it wasn't enough. I found reading quite helpful as it contributed a great deal in distracting my mind from all the disruptions. I read everything I could put my hands on. I continued reading books that I started months back but had never finished. On my iPad, I had at least half-a-dozen eBooks that I never finished. I realized there couldn't have been a better time to complete all of them.

A few of those books changed my perspective on life. They helped me in getting out of the loops my mind was in. They were about essential topics like happiness, change, motivation, meditation, and self-improvement. This memoir also includes my perceptions, observations, and learning that I absorbed through literature.

One of the books that changed my perspective on my understanding is *The Power of Now* by Echart Tolle. It helped me articulate what I was experiencing and feeling in earlier chapters of my life and shedding light on how I've been *organically* and subconsciously dealing with my current disruptions. I learned how my journey of dealing with disruption and rising above them was taking shape. Here is what I learned as it relates to my life.

I'm Not Frank

My mind is an instrument, a tool to be used for a specific task, and when the task is completed, I put it to rest. 80-90% of people's thinking is repetitive and useless. The mind becomes dysfunctional following a pattern of repetition, which may lead to self-harm. I observed how *Frank* works and how it causes a severe leakage of vital energy.

I have formed identities with *Frank* – that part of me that is always thinking of concepts, ideas, the past, and the future. It is essential to think constructively and positively. However, there could be huge problems when I identify myself with that thinking.

A mind is a tool. I can use it to create goals and further work to fulfill them. When I base my identity on it, I miss out on what it is designed to do. I prevent myself from seeing reality as it really is. Since the mind uses up vital energy, it drains from my critical resources that I can conserve and redeploy to different areas of my life so that I can work longer. It will allow my mind to be present for so I can value and enjoy the moment. It will help me engage myself in what I'm doing, which does not always involve the mind.

Identifying With Frank

It causes thoughts to become compulsive. Compulsive Thought – it seems to be a *badge of honor* that's given to somebody that thinks a lot. The reality is that we don't want to think more but effectively. We want to use Frank to think about the right things at the right time to help us be productive. Everything else should be in being who we are, and in doing, in acting, in reflecting, in being in the moment.

It's only from that place where I can get the most valuable and insightful information as feedback for my mind. It then allows me to work with it and optimize my activities. I can figure out what to do next with its help. It's done differently than how most people in society transact or carry themselves. In modern society, most people are trying to get to some destination, or they always have resentment with their past.

Some even overthink their past, and they feel that they can't do what they really want to do. Some people have a painful past, and letting go of it is always a challenge. Because of these hardships, the mind creates stories telling us why the future is better than *now*. It is also possible that the past might have held them back as they're continually identifying themselves with these stories. The thoughts that spawn from these identifications become compulsive.

Contain the Ego

To the ego, the present hardly exists, and thus, only the past and future are considered significant. Ego is a part of me that I was born with. Ego is a threat to one's success. Ego is an unhealthy belief in our own importance. It takes concern and turn it into obsession and turns confidence into arrogance. Ego sabotages our long-term goals, and it distracts us from achieving mastery in our craft or profession.

Ego shows up in my life when I experience success. After achieving something great that impresses people like getting promoted or getting industry recognition as one of the youngest executives in my industry, my ego leads me to believe that all future endeavors are likely to be a success. Instead of remaining focused and building upon previous success, I had the tendency to be overconfident about my abilities and take on too much. After a 25-year streak of success building new telcos and transforming legacy ones, I was convinced that I was invincible. I had all the confidence in the world that my startup would succeed and that all the upsides that I forecasted were going to materialize. I told you what really happened, right?!

The 2nd-way ego shows up in our life when you aspire to do something great. Ego gets busy in seeking approval from others around us. When I started up my digital innovation company, I spent a good part of my energy and time in promoting it. I was constantly updating our social media channels with news (big and small).

I was conducting interviews with trade magazines, presenting in industry conferences, talking to my network of professional contacts. I did an outstanding job selling the idea and getting approval on my idea. My ego was keeping me always asking what people are thinking about me. I preferred talking about what I was going to do, rather than actually doing it.

The irony was that I felt I was productive by doing all this talk and PR, but in actuality, I wasn't achieving the needed results. The 3rd way ego shows up in our life is when we experience failures or setbacks. It shows up just in time to safe face and dodge responsibility.

In an effort to defend our ego, we lose sight of what we worked for and ignore the work we've made to this point. In all three phases, ego distracts me from really doing the work and produce something that I can be proud of.

The ego focuses my attention on how people perceive me, which is detrimental if I'm trying to heal from the wounds of my disruptions. The more the ego makes me care about how I'm perceived, the farther I get from the truest highest version of myself. My ego will always be there. The more success I have, the more this ego will creep in, and the more it will try to outwit you.

Essentially, the ego tries to outwit me through various mechanisms. I tried to explore these mechanisms, so I can play the game better to understand who I really am. It enables me to value what is really crucial and not identify with the ego because the ego is *not me.*

I can feed the ego by attaching to the past or always thinking about the future where I want to be and not valuing what I have right now. In other words, it lacks gratitude. Eventually, I will believe my ego if I keep feeding it. So being present and being in the *now* means letting go of that ego. It means stepping out of mind. As I said, the mind is a tool. It's not who I am.

Consciousness

The way out of pain. The pain that I have is a form of non-acceptance, some form of unconscious resistance to reality. On the thought level, the resistance is some form of *judgment*. On the level of emotion, the resistance is some form of negativity. The intensity of the pain depends on the degree of resistance to the present moment.

This, in turn, depends on how strongly I identify with my mind – with Frank. The mind always seeks to deny the truth of the present and tries to escape from it. In other words, the more I identify with my mind, the more I suffered. The more I can honor and accept the now, the more I'm free of pain, suffering, and egoism of Frank.

Non-acceptance is not accepting things the way they are. I'm not talking about passively accepting and putting up with stuff you shouldn't be putting up with. I'm talking about understanding what's happening right now is what's happening right now. I'm not going to connect that in my mind to stories from my past or identifications that are ego-based to create resentment or anything disempowering. I would instead learn to accept things the way they are and recognize that my past is not who I am anymore. I must accept I'm no longer the corporate CEO, nor the well-off guy living the high life. The *ego* has given meaning to that, and it's causing me grief. It is actually amplifying the pain to internalize it further to root itself in me. Accept what's happening to me and do something positive about it. If I am willing to steer the situation at hand in a positive direction, I'm less likely to identify with that pain or feel it to that magnitude or connect to that negativity.

When I identify with that negativity and pain excessively, that part will root itself into my subconscious mind. Later on, when the ego needs to draw upon more power over me when something happens to me, it will relate back to that past pain and bring me back there for further feeding itself. Again, the ego is something that we've put together to help us grow and appreciate things.

Real appreciation and gratitude are being in the *now*, being in the moment, and understanding that all that really matters is this moment. When I value this moment, I create the neural pathways to appreciate the present, which I may see in different moments. The more I do that, the more I solidify those patterns, and the more I will value the *now*. This is where you'll find *happiness*.

Many people think that happiness will come sometime in the future when the conditions change from what they are right now. The reality is that the changing conditions also might not make you happy. It is because everywhere you go, you are who you are *right now*. How you do one thing is how you do everything.

If you no longer want to create pain for yourself and others and no longer want to add to the residue of past pain that still lives in you, don't create any more "time" to deal with the practical aspects of life. How do you stop creating time? Realize deeply that the *present moment* is all you have! All that ever exists is the present.

All that will ever exist is also your present. Time is something that we created as a construct, and it's valid. We can quantify it, we can explain it, we can work with it, and we shouldn't deny it. I look at time as something that I understand that exists. However, the most important thing is the one I'm doing right now, and the most important person is the one I'm talking to now. Five minutes from now, if I'm talking to someone else, that would be the most important person. All that ever existed is now. I have to become really present and aware now. Because it's from there, you show real gratitude, experiencing real emotions. It makes things more vibrant, improving your overall situation. As you hit your goals, you will value what you hit. I've been in stages of my life where I've been more focused on the future.

Therefore, I wasn't present to the moment, present to the now, and then when I got to the destination I was seeking, I didn't value it as much. When I look back at my childhood, it reminds me of how I valued certain moments.

Although they seemed simple moments, they were more joyous, valuable, and powerful. I recognized that's because everywhere I went, I was who I am. Therefore, if I'm not valuing this moment, when I get to my higher level of goal that I want to achieve, I'm not going to value it truly. I have to consciously and consistently value now.

Accept then Act

Whatever the present moment contains, learning to accept it as if I have chosen it is key. I work with it and not against it; I make it my friend and ally, not my enemy. I needed this in the dark tunnel to miraculously rise above my misery. The key is accepting what is happening right now and then acting from there. But how to accept that I'm dying? How to accept that there is no light at the end? The only way out is to be equipped to make better decisions because I'm basing it from my source energy – my connectedness to God – my purpose. I'm not basing the actions on fear, anger, resentment, or anything else that was constructed through time and past experiences and are stories generated by the mind for the ego. Have I ever experienced, done, thought, or felt anything *outside the Now*? Do I think I ever will? Is it possible for anything to happen or be outside the *now*? The answer is evidently *NO*! Nothing ever happened in the past; it occurs in the *now*.

Nothing will ever happen in the future; it will happen in the *now*. *Everywhere I go, there I am*. Energy always existed, it cannot be created, and it cannot be destroyed. However, it could change based on the projections of our internal reality. How we see things is how we think of them. Things change with thoughts, so our thoughts create things.

The thought is driven by energy. We require energy and passion for taking actions that matter to create things. If I'm not operating from the frame of *everywhere I go, there I am*, I'm not carrying with me the power that I'm capable of carrying through my journey daily to create what

I really want. It starts with the *now*. All negativity is caused by an accumulation of psychological time and denial of the present. Unease, anxiety, tension, stress, and worry are all forms of fear caused by too much thinking about the future and not paying enough attention to the present.

Guilt, regret, resentment, grievances, sadness, and bitterness are all forms of non-forgiveness caused by too much past and not enough present. If I'm holding on to any of these, I'm uncalibrated. If I start to remove these aspects, I'm not in the *now*. I'm centered and grounded in the *now*. One of the best ways to help me with these areas is to observe how I respond to different external stimuli as I carry myself throughout the day.

I ask myself – checklist-style – is my response based on any of these things? If they are, am I looking to the past situations, or am I looking too much into the future? Why would I not be valuing this moment? It is a humbling experience to realize that you have control over this and that the feelings that you have come from your mind.

It happens when the mind travels into these past and future periods and generates those emotions. When I become present to the *now*, my Frank goes away in the sense that such negative feelings go away. I realized that I cannot be both *unhappy and present in the now*. If I'm unhappy, I'm are not in the present. I must do things to bring myself back into the *now*. It could be done with things like meditation, connecting, and conversing with people.

Listen and understand them and value what they have to say. Work with the energy of the interaction. Other helpful activities might include sports, running, and playing golf. Some people are good at bringing others into the now – they are very present. Then, what I experience is pure joy, energy, and bliss at that moment due to that person's present energy projecting on to me.

Basically, they are facilitating my own present energy to come out. Wherever *I am, I'll be there,* totally. If I find I'm *here and now* intolerable, and it makes me unhappy, I have three options: Remove myself from the situation, change it, or accept it in its entirety.

If I want to take responsibility for my life, I must choose one of those three options, and I must decide now, then accept the consequences. No excuses, no negativity, and no psychic pollution! I must keep my inner space clear.

Forgetting the Past

I realized I don't need the past. I only refer to it when it is absolutely relevant to the present. I feel the power of this moment and the fullness of *being*. I feel your presence. I'm 50 years old now and have plenty of life experiences. Throughout those years, and especially the last two, I've experienced hardships and traumas.

Therefore, I must remain diligent in ensuring that I'm not forming an identity with those past situations. I'm essentially writing those stories in this book to give them an empowering meaning and purpose to help others. This way, I don't allow those hardships to wear me down. In fact, since I did that, I feel so much energized now, more than I ever thought I would.

I don't feel like things are holding me back as they used to a few months back, and most of it has to do by not associating with stories and identifications from my past. That doesn't mean I resist my past or don't appreciate it. I do it significantly. I see my past as a teacher. However, I let go of the emotions that hold me down and keep me from moving forward like excess baggage. In this way, I can be more present. Still, I can also carry into the future (which is the now) a lot more of lighter energy.

You can see people as they age. They give signs of being worn down and carrying heaviness. You can see it physically in their body. You can feel their energy holding on to their past. It's sad because they don't realize it most of the time. If you try to talk to them about it, they form such a deep identity with their past that it is hard for them to let go of it. They actually have to seek professional help.

I understand this about myself now that I don't want to end up in a situation where my story of who I'm and what I'm capable of is held back by the negativity of my past. I didn't have control over it and didn't understand how it worked, so I needed to let it go. It might be quite traumatic, but I have to make peace with it to move on and stay in the present.

Focus Less on the Future

On the flip side of living in my past, there is another dark side. It is to be too attached to my future. So now, my model is to set a goal and be really present in the current moment as I work toward that goal appreciating all areas of my life and understanding that I can appreciate those areas even more. By doing this, I'm making better decisions, instead of getting caught up in the process of trying to grind today for tomorrow. It happened to me in the past that when I got to my goals, I wasn't able to enjoy the fruits of my labor. For example, in 2009, one of the growth years of my career and income, I set a goal to buy a Mercedes SUV as my birthday gift if I achieve my corporate targets that year. I worked my butt off following my goal. I would have daydreams of the moment I'd put my hand on this new *toy*. When I achieved the goal and bought the car, I didn't really enjoy it as much as I've expected.

I failed to live in the now and started to chase in my mind my next goal. Same with travel. I made it a habit to travel with my wife and kids on a big trip every time I'd reach a certain level of income. I started traveling, and it took me a while to enjoy some of these exotic destinations because I was so looking forward to that day that I didn't value the *now*. When that *now* became that day that I was traveling, I didn't know how to be in it. I now understand that there is a dark side for being too attached to the past and too attached to the future.

Living the Moment

I found out by practice that when Frank was quiet from flooding me with fixed thoughts is when I was living the moment. By that, I mean when I focused intensely on the present. My reading glasses needed fixing, which required me to open up my tools box, find the right size screwdriver, shed light on the exact spot, then tighten the screw to fix the loose arm.

That was an intense experience requiring my full consternation and precise movements. As long as I was in that state of intense presence, I was free from fixed or negative thoughts. I was still yet highly alert at the moment. The instant my conscious attention sinks below a certain level, thoughts rush in. The mental noise returns, the stillness is lost, and I'm back in time.

In a sense, living the moment could be compared to waiting. There is a qualitatively different kind of waiting, one that requires my total alertness. Something could happen at any moment, and if I'm not absolutely awake and still, I will miss it. This is the kind of waiting I'm referring to.

It could be referred to as being prepared, active, or conscious waiting. Within my awareness now, there lies an opportunity. The problem is I don't see it because I'm too fixated on my past, and I'm too busy forming an identity around it. Or maybe, I'm thinking about something else I should be doing that I'm not valuing what's right now. It gets frustrating when I catch myself in this state because I can miss many opportunities in vital areas of my life. When I learned to be totally still, present, and aware, then opportunities stood out.

Sometimes, I could be out and about in a busy environment with a lot of people, and a person will stand out – almost glow. I'll go talk to them, and that's the person I was supposed to talk to. Those kinds of situations happen when I'm fully present or as present as I could be – they stand out. I don't know how it works. Perhaps it's the law of attraction.

These situations happen a lot to me in business. Some of the most profitable opportunities come to me while being in a place of actively waiting when I'm open and in the moment. When I'm present, all of a sudden, I see something that stands out, and its crystal clear what that means; it's a sign, and I follow it.

Many people are so imprisoned in their minds that nature's beauty does not exist for them. They acknowledge that a flower is pretty, but they do it in a mechanical mental labeling way. Because they are not still, not present, they don't truly see the flower, don't feel its essence and its holiness.

Similarly, they don't know themselves and don't feel their own essence and holiness.

Relevant Relationships

Relationships seem perfect for a while, such as when you are "in love," but invariably, that apparent perfection gets disrupted as arguments, conflicts, dissatisfaction, and emotional violence occur with increasing frequency. In looking back at my past relationships, I concluded that some of them failed during the times when I was not happy with who I was, when I was not at peace and couldn't see that there was more to me than my ego, my mind, and my body.

As the saying *"Everywhere I go there, I am"* came from that place. Relationships can be devastating – romantic or friendship relationships – especially if it doesn't come from a pure place. Because a lot of times, people get into relationships to fill a void, something missing in their lives.

In the earlier stages, this new person that they connect with fills these voids. However, when stuff starts to surface up, later on, things appear that they don't like about the new person. What happens is that they saw that person in a specific light, but now they are appearing differently or revealing some other aspects that were not visible before. People caught in their past start to blame that person. When in actuality, it's an opportunity because what the new person is really revealing the things that the other person doesn't like and love about themselves. It forces such people to avoid relationships instead of finding the wrong in them and correcting them. But how to correct such flaws in a relationship? The answer, in my humble opinion, is in being present and giving the other person all your attention ever more deeply into the *now*. When I'm in the *now,* I'm not getting attached to stories of the past or over-identifying with the future. This approach has helped me a lot with my current relationships.

Beyond Happiness and Pleasure, There Is Peace

In reading about happiness, one of the best comparisons I've seen is Robert Lustig's unique and articulate explanation of how happiness and pleasure are achieved in different ways.

"Pleasure and happiness a lot of people equate the two. Pleasure is short-lived. Happiness is long-lived. Pleasure is visceral. Happiness is ethereal. Pleasure is taking. Happiness is giving. Pleasure can be achieved with substances.

Happiness cannot be achieved with substances. Pleasure is experienced alone. Happiness is experienced in social groups. The extremes of pleasure all lead to addiction, yet there's no such thing as being addicted to too much happiness. Pleasure is dopamine, and happiness is serotonin. There's one thing that down-regulates serotonin, dopamine, so the more pleasure you seek, the unhappier you become. Las Vegas, Madison Ave, Wall Street, Silicon Valley, and Washington DC have very specifically confused and conflated the term happiness with the term pleasure so that you can buy happiness, and, in the process, we have become most decidedly unhappy."

Peace, in my view, is a higher state of being content. It does not rely on a certain aspect that if they exist, you'd be in peace, and if they don't, you won't be peaceful. I found myself seeking peace during and after my disruptions, not happiness. Maybe because the idea of feeling jolly was distant and overwhelming, my instinct gravitated toward peace. I wanted to go through my day in peace without pain, whether physical or emotional. *Living in the now* became my new way of life. Every time *Frank* started to play his tricks on me, I forced myself to gravitate back to the *now*.

13 - THE NEW ME

The Calm After the Storm

*I*t wasn't until the end of January 2020 – 12 months after the flood of disruptions that hit me – that I started to feel some normalcy in my life. The critical part of cancer treatment was successfully completed, with only four remaining chemo sessions for prevention and cleanup. I started to gain back weight and be healthy enough to do sports. I went back to practice my favorite sport, golf.

I regularly went out and about with friends to socialize and feel back the need to have fun. I started to do more intense work and take long term projects. By then, my kids had come back from college during the Christmas and End of Year Holidays. Life was brighter again!

One thing was clear in my mind; for sure, I was not the same person I was a year ago. The new me had many different characteristics. For starters, my ego was much humbler after all the bruises it went through. My tolerance for handling negative people or situations, or for "high-maintenance" acquaintances or colleagues went down to almost zero. I became focused on keeping my attention on the "now," on being "present in the moment." I stopped Frank from taking me back into my past or pushing in my imaginations of the future. Teddy became the center of my internal conversations. I realized that for quite some time, I kept Frank in the driver seat. Teddy was the impulsive, spontaneous, passionate, irrational voice that fed me ideas and decisions which always conflicted with Frank's logic, reserve, risk-averse, ego-preserving rationalization.

Throughout the struggle I've been through during my disruptions, and in reflecting back on my life, I realized that my "heart" was always in the right place but many times was not given the importance it deserved. It was because I used to value being the logical, egoistic, calculating jerk that I was.

I struggled throughout my adulthood in opening up to people, even to my wife of 22 years. Not for anything against them, but for a distorted, unrealistic, confusing belief that opening up my emotions would become a weakness that would render me at a disadvantage emotionally, socially, and even professionally. So, I kept my emotions for myself.

Power of Meditation

The new me mediated daily. I found the inner piece in taking my daily religious routine a couple of steps further and added meditation. By the beginning of March, I started a new 21-day meditation program for finding abundance in my life. This meditation changed me in many ways because its core matched profoundly with my inner desires.

The main idea of abundance is the experience in which all my needs are easily met, and my desires are spontaneously fulfilled. I know it's true that I'm balanced when I feel joy, help, happiness, a sense of purpose, and vitality in every moment of my existence. It is an overflowing fullness that infuses every facet of my life.

We never need to seek abundance. We simply need to notice and open up to what's already there and allow the blessings of God to flow through us. Each of us experiences abundance every day in the unbounded joy with child, the bright sunlight that fills the room as you open your eyes to a new morning - the many friends and family who are always there for you. Every day I would wake up early, do my morning rituals, bring my coffee to my desk, then start that day's abundance meditation. I would listen to the speech, do the day's exercise, close my eyes, focus on releasing today's intention, and release the mantra.

It is such a relaxing and enlightening activity that I passionately did every day. Mainly my intentions revolved around finding an abundance of money, love, and health and manifest them into my life. Few days after I started meditation, I signed a consulting contract for a short-term project with one of the largest companies in the country. This could very well be a coincidence, but I wanted to believe that it was not.

Day after day, the exercise and intentions went deeper and deeper into areas that I did not think this meditation would address. For instance, listing personal debts, sources of income, relationship with money, people who inspire me professionally, my shortcomings and flaws, my strengths, and the list goes on and on. I truly got fulfilled by this daily meditation spiritually and emotionally. In fact, I started to have a different perspective on life, gratitude, money, and joy.

Day 12 of the program happened to be the 14th of March, and it was titled: "Abundance and The Law of Intent and Desire." The guru asked to write down my three highest goals in life. My answers were money, joy, and love. To be specific on the last intention: Meet and live with a nice woman whom I love. That day's centering thought was, "I place my intention into the vast ocean of all possibilities and allow the universe to work through me." I felt good about the day's meditation and went through my day with vigor and excitement. Then the most amazing thing happened on the same day. I met the woman I've always knew existed but never met until that day. She was a dirty blond, stylish, cheerful, and had a unique charisma that grabbed my attention. We later dated then got engaged.

Was that fate? Was the universe listening? Did my intention got manifested that quickly?! Too many questions, with so little knowledge to answer them. All I can tell you is: I met the woman whom I plan to marry on the same day I set my intention to the cosmos to find love.

It was pure coincidence, or rather serendipity, that I met my woman. I was sitting in a bistro waiting for my car to be washed when a couple of friends showed up in the place. I asked them to join my table, and they did. A few minutes later, one of their close friends was walking around the place, they saw her, asked her to join us, and she did. We sat, the four of us shooting the breeze and laughing about the Coronavirus, as it was just a novel thing. We exchanged stories about the recent rainstorm Cairo never saw in a hundred years and other fun topics. We exchanged phone numbers and started to get to know each other. We kept on talking every day during the Corona lockdown, which started just a few days after. All of a sudden, the Corona pandemic became our friend.

Without it, we wouldn't have had so much free time on our hands to get to know each other. She lived in my neighborhood, where we're able to meet and do daily walks around the parks. One thing led to another, and there you have it. It was two people, matching on so many levels, enjoying each other's company, starting to envision a much more interesting life together as opposed to each on their own.

Destiny?

Our meeting was destiny. We each found what we were looking for and missing in a partner. She was sent into my life to give me what I've been missing and seeking all along, connecting and expressing my emotions. "Rumi" – one of the most famous poets of all time, who lived in the 13th century in Turkey and has been described as the most popular poet in the world – said the famous quote: "What you seek is always seeking you." One of the main reasons this lady was sent into my life was to show me how to unleash my suppressed feelings and articulate my emotions freely in any situation. I was not expressive of my feelings at all, most of my life. I have no issues talking in public. I can give a speech in an auditorium full of thousands of people for hours, telling them stories, make them laugh and cry, inspire them, or convince them of any topic. But if asked to talk about my emotions, I turn into a 5-year-old boy who is shy to say his name in front of two people!

She taught me how to be expressive of my emotions, how to bring my guard down, and how to speak my heart out. It was very difficult at first but started to get easier by practice. I recall the first real lesson she taught me – which was not planned – she asked me a simple question.

Why are you interested in knowing me? That was a few weeks after meeting her. I didn't know what to say. I froze, and for the next 45 minutes, I was the most uncomfortable 50-year-old man in the world. I fumbled, I didn't say a meaningful sentence, I had loads of emotions coming out but unfiltered, unorganized thoughts, I was really miles from my comfort zone. Noticeably, I made an effort to continue. I really wanted to let her know what I felt about her because I liked her and didn't want to short-change myself by not saying what was on my mind. By opening up and speaking about my emotions, I started to speak of emotions from years back that I've never articulated to anyone. Before long, I noticed a change in the way I expressed my emotions to my kids, family, and friends. I became more "emotional" and passionate speaking of feelings openly, something I rarely did.

This change was actually reflected in this book. If you read an earlier version of this book, you'd notice the big difference. Earlier versions were pathetic. It was an executive telling of boring facts-based stories with no emotions describing events, disruptions, and situations in a dull, uninviting way. I think by now, you've noticed that the book is rich in articulating the emotions and feelings I went through during my hardships.

Being part of my life, she gave me love and hope for a better future. She gave me an emotional "home" after being "homeless" for a long time. I also added to her life in many ways that she did not expect. I made her feel how talented, beautiful, positive, warm, considerate, fair, smart and grounded she is. I helped her regain faith in love after years of traumas. I helped her analyze her business and gave her ideas on how to transform her company into a faster-growing digital player. I made her believe in living with a husband again after settling with the idea that being single is best for her. The list goes on and on for both of us. The point is, I believe our meeting was never random; it was meant to happen so that each of us fills the gaps that the other provides in knowledge, affection, companionship, and synchronicity between heart, mind, and soul.

Pieces of the Puzzle

Each partner has in his or her mind the picture of the perfect relationship. Except each only has certain pieces of the puzzle for that perfect and happy relationship. When they find the other partner with the exact missing pieces of their puzzle, they "fit" and become "the one" for them because both their pieces form the perfect picture they each have in their mind. They might seem like an odd couple for outsiders.

But little do they know that each is the perfect fit for the other. When I met my woman, she had the exact pieces I was missing, and I had her's. She grounds me; she discharges me from my negative emotions and doubts. She sheds light on my blind spots. She exposes my weaknesses in situations where my brain either ignores or doesn't seize opportunities. She reminds me of what I need to keep doing and what I must avoid.

To her, I'm optimistic and can pacify and help ease her paranoia. I remind her of the beauty lying inside and outside her. I calm her nerves. I give her warmth and companionship. You see, I may get some of the missing pieces from another woman, but she has *all* the exact missing pieces in my perfect picture.

14 - JOURNEY INSIGHTS

I cannot believe how much I learned, grew, and matured in my journey of writing this book. The depth of emotions and sharpness in articulating my feelings and what I went through exceeded my expectations. I won't hide it; I've had moments of tears while writing many parts of this book.

They are not tears of sadness or pain, but tears of realization that I changed perspectives on many things I held in the past as defaults and matters of fact. No doubt, the biggest *loser* in this journey is my ego. I say loser from the perspective of old me. The new me believe that my ego now is where it should've been years ago.

Aha! Moments

As I'm approaching the conclusion of this great journey, I thought the best knowledge I can share with you is listing all the lessons, insights, learnings, reflections, revelations, or simply *aha-moments* that I've had. They are in no particular order.

* There is a bright side to any disruption. We don't see it in the beginning or during the darkest hours, but in the end, when you start to rationalize and accept the change, you'll see the bright side. Maybe then the reasons behind the disruption could become clearer.

* Disruption is a feeling as much as it is a matter of fact. The gap that exists between my expectations and reality is disruption.

* When I stepped outside my comfort zone, I began to change, grow, and transform. Being scared and paranoid sharpened all my senses and made me look for all possible outcomes and possibilities. It's in this frame of mind can one achieves things beyond their known capabilities.

* Focusing on finding the reasons behind traumas or disruptions takes too much energy and effort away from what's important, which is surfing your way back to the shore.

* Finding my synchronization between heart, mind, and soul is one of the most significant outcomes of my journey. I strive now to always be in synchronicity between what I'm feeling, thinking, and doing.

* My daily struggle is to try hard to stop being pushed by my fears and blocked by my insecurities. This is very difficult to do as Frank plays tricks on me all the time. One way out for me is praying and meditating. Another trick is to

allow my dreams to lead the way. To be honest, on some dark days, even allowing my dreams to lead the way is as big of a struggle as anything else. My only condolence is some days are up, some days are down, and some other days are just useless!

* I stopped letting the expectations and opinions of other people affect my decisions. It's my life, not theirs. I do what matters to me the most; I do what makes me feel alive and happy. If you let others tell you who you are, you are living their reality — not yours. There is more to life than pleasing people. There is much more to life than following others' prescribed path. There is so much more to life than what I experience right now.

* One of the side effects of believing in fate and destiny is your inability to be sure about anything. Nothing is for sure; nothing is for granted; nothing is a guarantee. We do the best we can, and most of the time, we have little control over the outcomes.

* COVID-19 has taught me that nothing to fear but fear itself. After being diagnosed and treated, I can vouch that the gap between what people warned me from and what actually transpired was big. Don't let the fears inside others impact your own conviction and attitude. I survived it in a much less painful way than others

have predicted. Seek and analyze real data, be connected to raw information, not opinionated views, while seeking second and third doctor opinions.

* Every day I strive to:

* **Be Passionate** is what makes you the person you want to become. If you want to become a doctor or an actor and don't have a passion for seeing your dreams through, you will never be able to achieve your goals. If you are passionate about bikes and love Harley Davidson, you will work hard to buy it. It's the passion that makes you love a sport. It is what makes victories and defeats important. It is the zest to improve. Most importantly, it is the passion that drives you to become a better person; it drives you to fall in love; pursue happiness, and the courage to dream big.

* **Be Rational:** Life is full of ups and downs. Things never stay at rest for long as the happenings of life gain control. The downs in life make you realistic and rational. The more difficult realities you witness, the more realistically you begin to think. It is what helps you understand the overhaul. Everyone needs to evaluate their aspirations. It is what keeps you grounded, especially if you are a dreamer like me. Dreamers do not limit their imagination to logical reasoning, and that is exactly where being

realistic becomes very critical.

* **Be Persistent:** Setting goals is a very easy task; accomplishing them is a whole lot different. Persistence is the key to success. You only fail to learn, and every time you fail, you learn a new way of how something shouldn't be done. Success is not an instance but a journey. If you really want to achieve your goals, you cannot do it without being persistent. Don't be ashamed to fail; instead, be ashamed of giving up. You can improve at anything in life if you persistently try to improve yourself. Persistence and passion go hand in hand. You cannot be passionate and fail in trying to be persistent at the same time. The same goes for your love life. If you are truly in love with someone, you just can't give up on the person. You try until there is any life left in the bond you share.

* **Be Committed:** The way we live up to our commitments is the way we respect ourselves and others. Failing to do so tampers our self-respect. Never make haste in making commitments; remember, there is no turning back. If you believe you have the passion for excelling in a particular field, commit to that passion, and work towards achieving it persistently.

* **Be Different:** Being different does not mean having a unique appearance or differing in the sense of actuality but with regards to innovation. Every person is unique in their own way, and diversity is what fuels innovation. Diversity is a beautiful thing, and I have been fortunate to have lived my life meeting people coming from different backgrounds. Our exposure to how people live differently, and how they do things differently has a great impact on our sense of innovation. Be somebody who always thinks outside the box and is willing to experiment. It's never about the resources at disposal, but rather how they are utilized.

* **Be a Trailblazer:** It is a characteristic I find common among all leaders. It requires a lot of courage to take the responsibility of leading from the front, but that is what allows you to exceed your own limits. Life will often be a mess, where you might find yourself stuck in a difficult situation. You must have the guts to crave a new path and be the first one to walk on it. To do so, you must welcome challenges and be committed to making it to the other side.

* **Be Daring:** Life tests our courage and valor regularly, and there are always consequences of how we react in those times. A daring person can make their way through any and every challenge. It is the weak who give-up and come in terms with reality, no matter how horrific it is. To bring change, being daring is

very important. You have to dare to stand against the status quo and be fearless to go alone against the crowd. There will be times when the result of your bravery leads to incurring losses, but in the long run, it is only going to make you a stronger person from the core.

During major change, it is the best time for the person to transform their life to a better, truer version of themselves. I found it an ideal time for me to re-evaluate my belief and value systems, "empty my cup" and refill it in the way I want. It was the perfect stage of my life to decide on who to keep and who let go of my friends and acquaintances. It was the right time for me to set the rules of engagement with my network of family and friends going forward. It was also the best time to decide on how I want my legacy to be. That's a deep and somewhat cliché statement. I used to hear a lot from older people or those with influence and a long history of success, but I never understood it. Well, now, I do.

Your legacy is what's going to be left after you leave this world. It is how your family and friends will remember you. Legacy becomes an important point in people's minds immediately after surviving trauma or a major life change. That's what happened to me. All of a sudden, my legacy became an obsession. What will I do to leave a good and memorable legacy? To answer this question, I went on a quest for knowledge around the subject, and before long, I found myself starting an exercise that took a life of its own and grew beyond my expectations. The end result of this exercise was a beautiful and logical model or recipe to reinvent me.

I needed to reinvent myself first before leaving a legacy, or at least that's what I believe. Here it is, my home-grown model for "personal transforming." They construct the acronym **RISE ABOVE**:

Rejuvenate your relationships with your support network (friends, family, colleagues, acquaintances, etc.) Get closer to the energy boosters. Those who are positive, honest, fun, interesting, and are value-add every time you interact with them. Keep a distance from the energy vampires, those who suck up positive energy with their negativity and pull you down. They are hard to deal with, and frankly, life is too short to know them. I know a number of such energy vampires with whom I keep interactions to the bare minimum if any.

Ignite your passions in your relationship with your partner, at work, and with your hobbies. Passion is what makes life worth living.

It's the euphoric feeling that takes over you to encourage you to do things with love and enjoyment. Re-evaluate your passions. If you had a passion for fishing, test yourself if you still have it. If you don't, it's time to find a new passion. It could be golf or tennis. Whatever it is, you must have something you're passionate about, and you must spend time enjoying it at least once a week. My passion is golf. I can't live without playing it at least once a week (I do at least three times!), and I do not know what I would've done without golf in my life. I really don't. It's a blessing to have a passion, and it's an even bigger passion to have the energy and patience to enjoy it. Find yours.

Scare yourself often by going outside your comfort zone and try new experiences. That's how you'll learn new skills and know more about yourself. I want to sign up for sky diving! I want to jump over Palm Jumeirah in Dubai. That thought, as much as it scares the banana out of me, I want to do it and write about it one day. Find your own scary thing. It could be theatre, whatever makes you absolutely outside your skin. It is really worth it.

Embrace change and find your own formula for dealing with it. Everyone has his/her own way of accepting change. Find yours and practice it.

Remember that you'll go through each stage of the SARA process, no matter what. The only constant in life is "change."

Accept anything life throws at you. Relax, you don't have control over anything, so why resist?! Remember that living in the now will allow you to focus only on the events that are taking place at the present moment and, hence, help you accept whatever is happening. When you expect nothing, anything that happens will exceed your expectations.

Beware of your blind spots. Test yourself to get ready for disruption. If you've been living a steady, uneventful, peaceful life, I recommend you do a "disruptions drill." Think of areas of your life where disruption could come from and identify contingency plans. For instance, what if my job gets downsized? Or my business goes bust? What if I lose my life partner? Test yourself on what your course of action will be.

Observe yourself and the environment. Many times, we don't spend enough time listening to our thoughts or deeply observe what is going on around us. I learned that most successful people spend at least 20 to 30 minutes every morning quiet and thinking and observing their surroundings. It gives them time to look at things from different perspectives.

Visualize where you want to be. I meditate 15 minutes every morning, and during that time, I try to visualize my goals and objectives. I visualize myself as a successful author of multiple books.

Evolve Accept the fact that you must evolve and strive to become a better, higher, truer version of yourself. Accept that your version today is not the same as ten years ago nor the one from five years into the future.

15 - RISE ABOVE ANYTHING

Corona, What Have You Done?

I don't think human beings have been disrupted in recorded history like they were with the Corona pandemic. It's hard to imagine that in the 21st century, 7.8 billion people buzzing non-stop 24/7/365 moving on foot, bicycles, in planes, trains, boats, automobiles, and motorcycles would freeze, literally freeze for three months! If you would've read this in a sci-fi novel ten years ago, you'd think it was cheesy.

The sheer disruption is of epic proportions, economically, socially, politically, medically, and humanly. After Corona, fear is no longer the same fear; stress is no longer the same stress; happiness is no longer the same happiness; caring for someone is no longer the same care; helping someone is no longer the same. Nothing is the same. If Corona is not the ultimate definition of disruption, then what is?

I believe now you can see a bit how interesting it was for me to write this book in the time I was writing it. I was writing about multiple personal disruptions in a short period of time, and as I was getting my life back to normal, I got hit, like the rest of the world, with Corona. No, literally, I was diagnosed with COVID-19! I laughed so hard that the doctor was a bit taken by my ambivalence. When I explained how my life was the last 12 months, he started to laugh with me! See, the moral of my story is if I can't control it, I can do nothing except to go with the flow, and so with the flow, I went.

Continuing the Journeys

The journeys I've been through in the last 12 months have been rich and eventful. I say journeys because they are a mesh of interdependent journeys, each on its own worth writing about. All of them combined to create the most memorable and life-changing endeavor I never imagined I'd go through. When "most" of the dust settled, and all the pieces fell in its places, I can see the track I took to get where I am now.

It was mostly unplanned, organic, driven by instinct, default beliefs, and trial and error. Did I rise above my disruptions? I can claim that I did indeed. However, I cannot claim that it was by design. I wanted to find peace and stop the pains, but to say I planned to heroically rise "gracefully" above it all to save the day and live happily ever after is a lie and an exaggeration.

I'm no hero for sure – as you've seen by now – but my only claim of achievement is that I faced my fears and refused to be beaten by failures, divorce, financial hardships, cancer, or COVID-19. I simply decided not to go without a big fight. While writing those last two chapters, life threw a couple of new disruptions at me.

My daughter's college financial aid was cut by more than half due to the economic crisis in the US, which means I will have to bear the difference in costs. In the meantime, I lost the job I had for the last few months due to the economic crisis caused by the Corona pandemic. My income got drastically cut, which put on hold (for now) plans to start a new life with the woman I love. Finally, I found out that I was infected with the COVID-19 virus and had to be treated and quarantined. Three and a half weeks into the treatment, I still have the symptoms with little progress. These hardships are taking a toll on me but not in the same intensity they would have a year ago. My tolerance and experience in dealing with uncertainty and fear have improved from the "beginner" to the "expert" level. I'm grateful than ever for every blessing I have. I count my blessings every day. I stopped taking anything for granted. I'm convinced now that I can only control what I can control; everything else will follow the forces of life, of gravity. For whatever I can't control, I'll plan for contingencies and do what-if scenarios, but I won't stress or worry much over the outcomes. I'll continue to do my meditation and morning routine – body, heart, and soul – and go through my day trying to manifest my daily intentions.

My new motto is: *"expect nothing and accept anything."* Any new disruption is welcomed. From now on, I'm capable of rising ***above anything***.

KHALED KHORSHID

www.ingramcontent.com/pod-product-compliance
Lightning Source LLC
LaVergne TN
LVHW041254080426
835510LV00009B/730